Contents

1 Introduction

Machine learning, a fundamental component of data science, empowers the automation of learning algorithms to effectively address classification and regression predictive challenges. In this upcoming publication, readers will gain insights into a plethora of methodologies, all utilizing the Python programming language, to proficiently engage in classical and ensemble machine learning. These techniques are specifically tailored for structured data predicaments.

Covering the entire spectrum of the machine learning process, this book is a comprehensive resource. From the initial stages of importing data to the final steps of creating robust models, each facet of the journey is meticulously explored. A wide array of topics is addressed, encompassing data importation of various formats such as CSV, Excel, and SQL databases into the Python environment. Once data resides within your workspace, the text delves into critical processing steps: encompassing data subset selection, imputation of missing or null values, outlier treatment, normalization methods, advanced feature engineering, adept data type conversions, and the pivotal task of data balancing.

As you progress, the book navigates the intricacies of data exploration, guiding readers to extract valuable insights that inform subsequent modeling decisions. By fostering a deeper understanding of the data, one can make informed assumptions, subsequently enhancing the data processing and modeling endeavors.

A focal point of the book is its comprehensive coverage of supervised classical machine learning techniques. Both regression and classification scenarios are addressed, incorporating a rich selection of tools such as linear regression, decision trees, random forests, support vector machines, and naive Bayes methods. The volume also thoroughly tackles the intricate art of ensemble modeling, an advanced technique that amalgamates various models to extract enhanced predictive power.

By the book's conclusion, readers will have acquired proficiency in executing machine learning procedures from the ground up, adeptly applying them to both regression and classification challenges using the Python programming language. This book stands as a comprehensive resource, poised to empower enthusiasts and professionals alike with the skills to harness the potential of machine learning for a myriad of real-world applications.

1.1 Brief Explanation of Machine Learning

At its core, machine learning is a sophisticated methodology that harnesses the power of optimized learning procedures to imbue machines with the capacity to perform targeted tasks. This capacity is cultivated through a meticulous analysis of past experiences and accumulated data. Within this realm, we delve into a specific and crucial facet known as *supervised learning*.

Supervised learning constitutes a pivotal subset of machine learning, characterized by its emphasis on training machines to unravel intricate patterns and relationships hidden within data. This is achieved by presenting the machine with a curated dataset, each entry comprising an input object coupled with its corresponding expected output. This set of meticulously labeled examples serves as the foundation upon which the machine constructs its learning framework.

The essence of supervised learning lies in its objective: the machine endeavors to develop an algorithm that can accurately map inputs to their respective outputs, essentially emulating the desired function. The training process involves fine-tuning the machine's internal mechanisms to minimize errors and discrepancies between predicted outputs and actual results. Through iterative refinement, the machine incrementally sharpens its ability to generalize from the training data, paving the way for robust predictions on new, unseen data.

This symbiotic dance between input and output encapsulates the essence of supervised learning. The machine learns to discern intricate patterns and correlations within the data, equipping it to extrapolate these insights to previously unseen scenarios. Ultimately, the goal is to cultivate a machine capable of making accurate predictions and informed decisions, thus transforming raw data into actionable knowledge.

In the subsequent sections of this publication, we delve deeper into the intricacies of supervised machine learning. We unravel the mechanics of training algorithms, explore diverse techniques to evaluate model performance, and unveil the nuances of optimizing model parameters. By mastering the principles and practices of supervised learning, readers will gain a robust foundation to harness the potential of this powerful paradigm in real-world applications.

1.2 Typical Processes and Structures

In the realm of machine learning research, a meticulous process underscores each machine learning algorithm, serving as a guiding framework for crafting effective solutions. The algorithm itself presents a plethora of choices that researchers encounter during solution development.

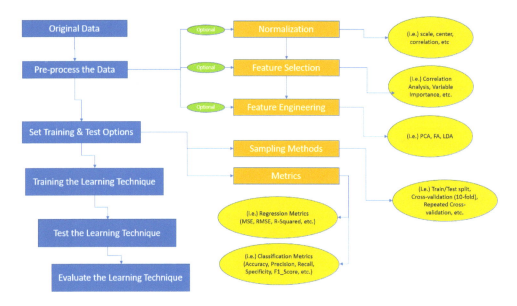

Figure 1: A schematic representation of a typical supervised learning process.

Figure 1 illustrates the complexity entailed in training, testing, and evaluating a supervised machine learning model. Beyond the model's core technique, the entire algorithm's architecture must be skillfully constructed to yield optimal results. Although the illustration depicts the training of a singular model, it effectively conveys the myriad options nested within the algorithmic structure, each contributing to the quest for superior performance.

Amidst the process, discernible choices emerge, offering researchers the flexibility to tailor the machine learning algorithm to specific needs. It is imperative to recognize that this depiction primarily exemplifies an algorithm utilizing a singular machine learning technique. For comprehensive insights into conducting machine learning modeling, readers are directed to the Classical Machine Learning Modeling section, where the delineated process will be further expanded upon.

Crucially, it must be acknowledged that a solitary algorithm is insufficient to navigate the realm of machine learning research. To genuinely evaluate the optimal performance, a minimum of three algorithms per model technique is necessary. This implies the requisite training and testing of nine algorithms in total.

To unveil the most effective modeling technique and algorithm holistically, adherence to a rigorous process akin to that depicted in Figure 2 is crucial. Each algorithm should advance sequentially, with Algorithm #1 encompassing steps like (1) utilizing original data, (2) data preprocessing involving normalization (e.g., scaling and centering), (3) training and testing configurations (e.g., train/test split and 10-fold cross-validation), (4) training and testing a minimum of three learning techniques, and (5) meticulous evaluation of these techniques.

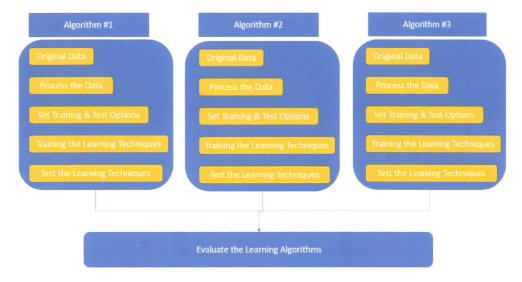

Figure 2: Machine Learning Research Process

Algorithm #2 introduces nuanced modifications, incorporating additional mechanisms. For instance, (1) original data, (2) data preprocessing involving normalization and correlation analysis, (3) feature selection via correlation analysis, (4) training and testing configurations, (5) training and testing multiple learning techniques, and (6) comprehensive evaluation.

Algorithm #3 further refines the process, infusing advanced mechanisms. It includes elements like (1) original data, (2) data preprocessing involving normalization and correlation analysis, (3) feature selection through variable importance assessment, (4) feature engineering employing Principal Component Analysis (PCA), (5) training and testing configurations, (6) training and testing diverse learning techniques, and (7) meticulous evaluation.

Upon training, testing, and evaluating the learning techniques within each algorithm, the optimal method from each algorithm can be discerned. Subsequently, a final assessment aids in identifying the overall optimal approach from the ensemble of algorithms. This comprehensive methodological structure underscores the meticulous approach necessary to yield robust and insightful results in the realm of machine learning research.

1.3 Types of Problems

Embarking on the journey of developing a machine learning solution brings forth an array of distinct problem categories that warrant consideration. Among these are:

- Classification
- Regression
- Time Series
- Clustering

In the ensuing pages, our focus crystallizes upon the two most recurrent domains in the landscape of machine learning research for (1) classification and (2) regression type problems.

1.3.1 Classification

Functioning in alignment with its nomenclature, classification is a pivotal technique that entails categorizing data with the ultimate aim of engendering accurate predictions. Firmly entrenched within the realm of supervised learning, classification unleashes its predictive prowess through a dedicated classification model, fortified by a robust learning algorithm.

The quintessential indicator for the need of a classifier materializes when confronted with a categorical or factor-based output variable. In certain scenarios, it becomes essential to engineer such a categorized output variable to suit the data, thereby reshaping the problem-solving task at hand. In such cases, the strategic deployment of conditional statements and iterative loops augments the arsenal of problem-solving techniques.

1.3.2 Regression

Regression analysis, a cornerstone of machine learning, epitomizes the art of prediction. Nestled within the realm of supervised learning, this paradigm hinges on the symbiotic training of algorithms with both input features and corresponding output labels. Its raison d'être lies in its aptitude for delineating the intricate relationships that interlace variables, thus unraveling the impact of one variable upon another.

At its core, regression analysis harnesses mathematical methodologies to prognosticate continuous outcomes (y), predicated on the values of one or more predictor variables (x). Among the pantheon of regression analyses, linear regression emerges as a stalwart due to its inherent simplicity and efficacy in forecasting.

1.3.3 Other Types of Problems

In tandem with classification and regression, this text ventures into the intriguing domains of time series analysis and clustering:

Time Series: A chronological sequence of observations underscores time series data. Forecasting within this realm involves marrying models with historical data to anticipate forthcoming observations. Central to this process are lag times or lags, which temporally shift data, rendering it ripe for supervised machine learning integration.

Clustering: Deftly positioned within the domain of unsupervised learning, clustering emerges as a potent technique for unraveling latent structures within data. Dispensing with labelled responses, unsupervised learning methods strive to discern underlying patterns and groupings that permeate a dataset.

It is paramount to note that this book primarily centers on techniques and methodologies tailored to tackle supervised classification and regression problems. By honing these foundational approaches, readers will glean insights into orchestrating effective solutions for a gamut of real-world challenges.

1.4 Organization of the Book

The organization of this book is meticulously structured to usher readers through a systematic journey of mastering machine learning in Python. Each chapter serves as a distinct waypoint in this transformative expedition:

- **Chapter 2: Preparing the Ground for Success:** In this chapter, you will be equipped with essential instructions to ready your computer with the requisite tools indispensable for executing the code examples woven seamlessly throughout the book. A comprehensive guide awaits in Chapter 2, facilitating a seamless transition into the realm of practical implementation. *(Refer to Chapter 2: Preparing the Ground for Success.)*

- **Chapter 3: Navigating the Data Landscape** The art of connecting with diverse data sources takes center stage in this chapter. Chapter 3 comprehensively navigates the process of establishing connections to an array of data repositories. *(Refer to Chapter 3: Navigating the Data Landscape.)*

- **Chapter 4: The Dance of Data Preprocessing:** The heart of data preprocessing is unveiled in Chapter 4, where you will immerse yourself in the intricacies of handling missing values, taming outliers, and orchestrating data scaling. Beyond these fundamentals, this chapter delves into advanced techniques such as feature selection and engineering. *(Refer to Chapter 4: The Dance of Data Preprocessing.)*

- **Chapter 5: Unveiling Data through Exploration:** Embarking on a journey of data exploration, Chapter 5 serves as your compass to unravel the rich information concealed within datasets. By mastering these techniques, you'll glean invaluable insights into the datasets' nuances and intricacies. *(Refer to Chapter 5: Unveiling Data through Exploration.)*

- **Chapter 6: Embracing Classical Machine Learning Techniques:** Chapter 6 heralds the unveiling of a plethora of classical machine learning techniques tailored for both regression and classification challenges. You will traverse the intricacies of these methodologies, developing a robust toolkit to tackle real-world problems. *(Refer to Chapter 6: Embracing Classical Machine Learning Techniques.)*

- **Chapter 7: The Symphony of Ensemble Modeling:** In the realm of Chapter 7, the concept of ensemble modeling takes center stage. By amalgamating multiple trained models, you'll uncover the potential to magnify predictive prowess and elevate model performance. *(Refer to Chapter 7: The Symphony of Ensemble Modeling.)*

- **Chapter 8: Decoding Model Evaluation:** Guided by the principles of Chapter 8, you'll navigate the nuanced art of interpreting performance results for trained classifiers and regressors. This chapter encapsulates best practices to derive actionable insights from your models. *(Refer to Chapter 8: Decoding Model Evaluation.)*

- **Chapter 9: Conclusion and Reflection:** As the expedition draws to a close, Chapter 9 offers a moment of reflection. Here, final remarks encapsulate key takeaways, underscoring the transformative journey undertaken throughout the book. *(Refer to Chapter 9: Chapter Conclusion and Reflection.)*

This structural design ensures a coherent and progressive exploration of machine learning in Python, culminating in your mastery of its principles and practical application.

2 Preparing the Ground for Success

A solid foundation is the bedrock of success, and this holds true in the world of Python programming. As you embark on your journey into the realm of data manipulation, analysis, and visualization with Python, the first crucial stride is to create a robust and optimized environment on your local machine. This chapter serves as your guiding light, leading you through a series of meticulously crafted steps to set up your environment for harnessing the full power of the Python programming language. By adhering to these carefully curated guidelines, you'll pave the way for a seamless and productive experience that sets the stage for your Python programming endeavors.

The journey commences with a fundamental checklist, meticulously designed to fine-tune your environment for Python programming excellence. We will escort you through each step, demystifying the installation of essential components that comprise the very backbone of your programming arsenal. The beauty of this approach lies in its accessibility; we've made sure that even newcomers to the world of Python can follow along effortlessly.

Whether you're taking your first tentative steps into the Python universe or gearing up for more intricate endeavors, dedicating time to this preparatory phase is akin to investing in your own success. The upcoming chapters will take you through complex analyses, data transformations, machine learning models, and visualizations. But all these exploits stand on the shoulders of a well-prepared environment. So, let's dive headfirst into the meticulous process of fortifying your local machine, a critical step towards attaining Python programming excellence.

2.1 Installing Python and IDLE

Your journey into the dynamic world of Python programming commences with a pivotal installation step: ensuring the presence of two fundamental components — Python and Jupyter Notebook. These tools stand as the cornerstone of your programming environment, collectively enabling you to tap into the unparalleled potential of the Python language. It's through the harmonious interplay of Python and Jupyter Notebook that you'll have the means to explore, analyze, and visualize data with precision and finesse. So, before embarking on your data-driven voyage, let's take a comprehensive look at the installation process that forms the bedrock of your Python programming endeavors in Jupyter Notebook.

2.1.1 Installing Python

To prepare the canvas for your forthcoming Python programming odyssey, it's imperative to lay the groundwork by installing a specific version of Python: Python 3.5 or lower. Ensuring a seamless installation process involves the following steps:

1. Initiate your journey by navigating to the following link: https://www.python.org/downloads/

2. On this web page, you'll find various Python versions available for download, categorized by different operating systems. Your task is to select the Python 3.5 or lower version that corresponds to your specific system.

3. Once you've selected the appropriate version, proceed with the download by clicking on the provided link.

   - For Windows: https://www.python.org/downloads/windows/
   - For macOS: https://www.python.org/downloads/mac-osx/

Embracing Python version 3.5 or lower in your installation journey stands as a pivotal juncture in ensuring harmonious compatibility with the tools and techniques that will be unveiled in the chapters ahead. This version serves as the cornerstone upon which we'll build a sturdy and proficient Python programming environment, poised for the exploration of data-driven realms in Jupyter Notebook.

2.1.2 Installing Jupyter

Positioned as your command center, Jupyter Notebook stands as the conduit to an enriched Python programming experience, providing an intuitive interface that elevates your journey. Acquiring Jupyter Notebook is a seamless process, guided by the following straightforward steps:

1. Initiate your journey by simply following the link thoughtfully embedded in the title above [**Jupyter**].
2. Upon arrival at the designated page, your attention will be drawn to a prominently displayed table, adorned with the assertive label "DOWNLOAD."
3. Directly beneath this bold proclamation, a conspicuous "INSTALL NOW" button extends an inviting invitation. Inevitably, you'll find yourself clicking this button, thus setting your course in motion.
4. Your next destination presents an array of Jupyter Notebook downloads, thoughtfully tailored to cater to diverse operating systems: Windows, Linux, and macOS. Your task is to select the version that impeccably aligns with your system's identity.
5. With your selection made, the gears of your Jupyter Notebook installation will engage, orchestrating the acquisition of this pivotal piece of software and heralding the beginning of an enriched Python programming expedition.

The installation of Jupyter Notebook equips you with a user-friendly interface that hosts an array of tools and features designed to streamline your coding endeavors, empower your data analysis pursuits, and render your visualization tasks more impactful. With Python and Jupyter Notebook seamlessly integrated into your programming sphere, you're poised to embark on your coding odyssey with an arsenal of potent resources at your disposal, poised to make your journey one of productivity and discovery.

2.2 Installing Python Modules

As you embark on your enthralling journey through the realms of Python programming and machine learning, arming yourself with indispensable Python modules emerges as a pivotal step. These modules are the foundational building blocks that empower you to harness the boundless potential encapsulated within Python's capabilities. The process of installing these modules is straightforward and seamless, ensuring that you have the necessary tools at your disposal to navigate the complexities of your programming odyssey.

To commence this empowering process, let these steps guide you through the installation and configuration of the essential Python modules. Although not an exhaustive list of the modules that will prove invaluable throughout your journey, the examples presented here elucidate the procedure of module installation in Python:

```python
import sys

# Install and import the 'pandas' module
if 'pandas' not in sys.modules:
    !pip install pandas
import pandas as pd

# Install and import the 'numpy' module
if 'numpy' not in sys.modules:
    !pip install numpy
import numpy as np
```

By substituting the module names in the code snippet above and executing it, you will initiate the seamless installation of the specified modules directly into your Python distribution. This meticulous process ensures that you're poised with the requisite tools, empowering your programming endeavors with the necessary resources.

With Python and your preferred IDE as your unwavering foundation and the indispensable modules seamlessly integrated into your environment, the captivating universe of Python programming and machine learning unveils itself to you. Your voyage towards mastery stands at the threshold, beckoning you to dive in with fervor.

A Quick Note: *Persistence Paves the Way!* It's imperative to acknowledge that the path of module installation may not always unfold without a minor hiccup or two on the initial try. Even experienced practitioners find themselves faced with challenges during this phase.

When embarking on the intricate terrain of module installation, be prepared to navigate a few twists and turns. Certain modules might necessitate several installation attempts, and compatibility hurdles specific to your operating system could surface. Amidst these challenges, take solace in the fact that you're not alone.

The very essence of learning resides in the expedition itself. Conquering these challenges doesn't just enrich your technical acumen but also forges the patience and tenacity requisite for success. Embrace the iterative nature of this process, keeping in mind that each small victory signifies a stride forward on your voyage of exploration and growth.

2.2.1 Troubleshooting Python Installation Woes

The journey towards achieving a seamless Python installation is accompanied by its own set of twists and turns. As you navigate the intricate terrain of Python module installation, you may find yourself facing a few unexpected roadblocks. However, rest assured that these challenges are not insurmountable. In fact, there are strategies at your disposal to navigate these hurdles with confidence. While certain issues might necessitate more in-depth investigation and tailored solutions, the steps outlined below can significantly assist you in circumventing common installation pitfalls.

While the process of installing Python modules might occasionally throw you a curveball, there's no need to be disheartened. Instead, consider the following strategies that can help you triumph over common obstacles:

2.2.2 Exploring Different Python Versions:

In the face of uncertainty or compatibility issues, delving into the realm of different Python versions can often hold the key to unlocking solutions. Embracing the strategy of installing an alternative version and seamlessly integrating it with your Python environment has the potential to offer a fresh perspective, effectively addressing any installation challenges you may encounter.

Embark on your exploration of Python versions with the following options in mind:

- Python 3.9.7 for Windows
- Python for macOS

Transitioning to a different Python version within your Python environment is a straightforward process, outlined as follows:

1. Access the settings or preferences within your Python environment.
2. Look for the Python version or interpreter settings.
3. Within the settings, locate the option to change or select a different Python version.
4. Make your selection from the available Python versions.
5. Don't forget to apply your changes.

Venturing into the world of diverse Python versions opens up a realm of possibilities for surmounting installation obstacles. This strategic approach can infuse a breath of fresh air into your efforts and potentially lead to smoother installation experiences, ultimately enhancing your journey into the world of Python programming.

3   Navigating the Data Landscape

Embarking on the captivating journey of data importation within the realm of Python opens up a myriad of pathways and possibilities. This pivotal chapter serves as your compass, guiding you through a diverse array of techniques designed to effortlessly usher data files into the heart of your Python environment. Here, you'll find a treasure trove of practical methods to not only import external data but also leverage the wealth of preloaded datasets nestled within your Python distribution and specialized libraries.

As you navigate the intricate landscape of data importation, you'll unearth an invaluable toolkit of insights and skills. The strategies unveiled here will empower you to seamlessly weave data from various sources into your analytical endeavors. Whether you're a seasoned data wrangler or a newcomer to the realm of Python, this chapter stands as an indispensable resource, illuminating the pathways to harmoniously integrate data into your explorations.

Imagine harnessing the capability to effortlessly draw in data from a plethora of sources, transforming your Python environment into a dynamic hub for data-driven insights. From structured databases to raw CSV files, this chapter equips you with the tools to bring them all under your analytical umbrella.

So, prepare to embark on a transformative journey—armed with these techniques, your Python environment will become a gateway to the intricate world of data, setting the stage for your future analyses, discoveries, and a deeper understanding of the datasets that shape our world.

3.1   Unveiling Pythons's Native Treasures

The odyssey begins with a delightful discovery of Python's inherent wealth of data. Upon installing Python, a generous trove of datasets eagerly awaits your exploration. To unlock these treasures, the Python ecosystem comes to your aid.

```python
# List available datasets
from sklearn.datasets import load_iris

data = load_iris(as_frame=True)
data.frame.head()
```

```
##    sepal length (cm)  sepal width (cm)  ...  petal width (cm)  target
## 0                5.1               3.5  ...               0.2       0
## 1                4.9               3.0  ...               0.2       0
## 2                4.7               3.2  ...               0.2       0
## 3                4.6               3.1  ...               0.2       0
## 4                5.0               3.6  ...               0.2       0
##
## [5 rows x 5 columns]
```

The command above unveils an array of datasets accessible through Python libraries like Scikit-Learn. A glance at the displayed dataset offers a mere glimpse into the rich array of choices presented before you.

Amid this treasure trove, the `seaborn` library stands as a favorite. It extends an intriguing invitation to access various datasets, allowing you to explore and analyze them freely. This invaluable resource will accompany us throughout the book, serving as a beacon to illuminate a myriad of examples.

To fully grasp the potential of these treasures, let's beckon a specific dataset, the illustrious `iris` dataset. Begin your expedition by invoking the Python libraries and summoning forth your chosen dataset:

```python
# Import necessary libraries
import seaborn as sns

# Load the iris dataset
iris = sns.load_dataset("iris")
iris.head()
```

```
##     sepal_length  sepal_width  petal_length  petal_width  species
## 0            5.1          3.5           1.4          0.2   setosa
## 1            4.9          3.0           1.4          0.2   setosa
## 2            4.7          3.2           1.3          0.2   setosa
## 3            4.6          3.1           1.5          0.2   setosa
## 4            5.0          3.6           1.4          0.2   setosa
```

This glimpse into the heart of the `iris` dataset serves as a prelude to the extensive explorations that await you within Python's diverse world of data. As you venture deeper into this realm, you'll find that each dataset carries a unique story, waiting for you to uncover its insights and unravel its mysteries.

3.2 Mastering CSV Files

A CSV file, which stands for "Comma-Separated Values," is a widely used file format for storing and exchanging tabular data in plain text form. In a CSV file, each line represents a row of data, and within each line, values are separated by commas or other delimiters, such as semicolons or tabs. Each line typically corresponds to a record, while the values separated by commas within that line represent individual fields or attributes. This simple and human-readable format makes CSV files highly versatile and compatible with a wide range of software applications, including spreadsheet programs, database management systems, and programming languages like Python. CSV files are commonly used to share data between different systems, analyze data using statistical software, and facilitate data integration and manipulation tasks.

CSV files stand as the quintessential medium for data interchange. Their simplicity and compatibility make them a go-to choice for sharing and storing tabular data. Here's where Python's finesse comes into play. With Python's built-in `csv` module as your trusty companion, you can seamlessly import CSV files into your Python realm, transforming raw data into actionable insights.

```python
import csv

# Define the path to your CSV file
csv_file = "./data/Hiccups.csv"

# Open and read the CSV file
with open(csv_file, mode='r', newline='') as file:
    reader = csv.reader(file)
    for row in reader:
        print(row)
```

```
## ['Baseline', 'Tongue', 'Carotid', 'Other']
## ['15', '9', '7', '2']
## ['13', '18', '7', '4']
## ['9', '17', '5', '4']
## ['7', '15', '10', '5']
## ['11', '18', '7', '4']
```

```
## ['14', '8', '10', '3']
## ['20', '3', '7', '3']
## ['9', '16', '12', '3']
## ['17', '10', '9', '4']
## ['19', '10', '8', '4']
## ['3', '14', '11', '4']
## ['13', '22', '6', '4']
## ['20', '4', '13', '4']
## ['14', '16', '11', '2']
## ['13', '12', '8', '3']
```

This code snippet demonstrates how Python can effortlessly handle CSV files. It opens the CSV file, reads its contents, and prints each row of data. With Python's flexibility and the `csv` module's functionality, you have the power to manipulate, analyze, and visualize CSV data with ease.

The beauty of importing CSV files with Python lies in the seamless transition from raw data to structured data ready for analysis. Python's robust libraries, such as Pandas, provide powerful tools for data manipulation and exploration. As you master the art of importing CSV files, you're equipping yourself with a foundational skill that sets the stage for powerful data-driven discoveries.

3.3   Harnessing SAV Files

An SAV file, commonly known as a "SAVe" file, is a data file format frequently associated with the Statistical Package for the Social Sciences (SPSS) software. SAV files are designed to store structured data, encompassing variables, cases, and metadata. This format is widely favored in fields like social sciences, psychology, and other research domains for data storage and analysis. SAV files encapsulate crucial information such as variable names, labels, data types, and values, alongside the actual data values for each case or observation. Researchers rely on these files to conduct intricate statistical analyses, perform data manipulation, and generate reports within SPSS. Furthermore, SAV files can be seamlessly imported into various data analysis tools and programming languages, including Python, using libraries like `pandas`, thereby ensuring cross-platform compatibility and broadening the scope of data analysis possibilities.

Incorporating data housed in SAV files into your Python journey is a straightforward process, thanks to the versatile `pandas` library, which offers robust support for diverse data file formats, including SAV files. This powerful library is your gateway to efficient data manipulation and analysis.

```python
import pandas as pd

# Define the path to your SAV file
sav_file = "./data/ChickFlick.sav"

# Read the SAV file into a Pandas DataFrame
chickflick = pd.read_spss(sav_file)

# Display the first few rows of the dataset
print(chickflick.head())
```

```
##    gender                film  arousal
## 0    Male  Bridget Jones's Diary     22.0
## 1    Male  Bridget Jones's Diary     13.0
## 2    Male  Bridget Jones's Diary     16.0
## 3    Male  Bridget Jones's Diary     10.0
## 4    Male  Bridget Jones's Diary     18.0
```

This Python code snippet showcases how you can effortlessly handle SAV files. It reads the SAV file into a Pandas DataFrame, providing you with a structured data format for analysis. With Pandas' extensive functionality, you can perform data manipulations, explorations, and visualizations with ease.

The `pandas` library's capabilities extend far beyond SAV files, offering compatibility with various other data formats commonly encountered in data manipulation and analysis. As you become adept at importing SAV files with Python, you're honing a versatile skill that equips you to seamlessly integrate diverse data sources into your analytical endeavors. This proficiency positions you to extract meaningful insights from a multitude of data formats, making you a data-driven decision-maker of exceptional competence.

3.4 Wrangling XLSX Files

Working with XLSX files in Python is a seamless process. The `pandas` library provides excellent support for importing and manipulating Excel files, making it a valuable tool for data analysis and manipulation directly within Python.

To explore the world of XLSX files in Python, follow these steps:

1. **Import the pandas Library**: Start by importing the `pandas` library to access its powerful functionality for handling Excel files.

2. **Set Your Working Directory**: Ensure that your current working directory corresponds to the location of your XLSX file. This step ensures that Python can locate and access the target Excel file.

3. **Import with `read_excel()`**: Now, you're ready to import the XLSX file. Use the `read_excel()` function, specifying the file's path within the function. This action allows you to access the dataset contained within the Excel file.

By following these steps, you can seamlessly incorporate XLSX files into your Python analyses, enhancing your data manipulation and exploration capabilities.

```python
import pandas as pd

# Define the path to your XLSX file
xlsx_file = "./data/Texting.xlsx"

# Read the XLSX file into a Pandas DataFrame
texting = pd.read_excel(xlsx_file)

# Display the first few rows of the dataset
print(texting.head())
```

```
##    Group  Baseline  Six_months
## 0      1        52          32
## 1      1        68          48
## 2      1        85          62
## 3      1        47          16
## 4      1        73          63
```

This Python code snippet demonstrates how to work with XLSX files using the `pandas` library. It reads the XLSX file into a Pandas DataFrame, providing you with a structured data format for analysis. With Pandas' extensive capabilities, you can easily manipulate, explore, and visualize the data.

Now, let's take a moment to understand what XLSX files are. An XLSX file, short for "Excel Open XML Workbook," is a modern file format used to store structured data and spreadsheets. It has been the default file format for Microsoft Excel since Excel 2007. XLSX files are based on the Open XML format, which is a standardized, open-source format for office documents. These files contain multiple sheets, each comprising rows and columns of data, formulas, and formatting. XLSX files have gained popularity due to their efficient data storage, support for larger file sizes, and compatibility with various software applications beyond Microsoft Excel, making them an ideal choice for data interchange and analysis.

3.5 Exploring Further Avenues

While this chapter provides insights into data importation techniques, Python offers an expansive landscape of possibilities for data manipulation. The examples mentioned here only scratch the surface. More advanced data importation and manipulation methods await exploration in our forthcoming book—*Advanced Application Python*.

Intriguingly, Python accommodates numerous other pathways for importing and working with data, some of which we briefly touch upon here. Keep in mind that we will delve deeper into these methods in our advanced guide:

- **Web Scraping with Requests**: Python's `requests` library empowers you to retrieve data from webpages directly into your Python environment. This technique can be valuable for scraping data from online sources, enabling you to work with real-time and dynamic information.

- **Making API Requests for Data**: Python's `requests` library, along with specialized libraries like `requests-oauthlib` or `http.client`, equips Python with the ability to make API requests. This allows you to fetch data from various web services. This approach is particularly useful when dealing with APIs that provide structured data, such as JSON or XML.

- **Connecting to Databases**: For scenarios where your data resides in databases, Python's `sqlite3`, `SQLAlchemy`, or other database connectors open doors to connect to and interact with databases. This can be invaluable when working with large datasets stored in database systems, granting you the ability to fetch, analyze, and manipulate data with the power of Python.

As you journey deeper into the realm of Python programming and data manipulation, these advanced techniques will serve as valuable tools in your arsenal, expanding your capabilities and horizons in the world of data science and analysis.

4 The Dance of Data Preprocessing

Welcome to the captivating world of data preprocessing in Python. Having successfully brought your data into the spotlight, the next step is to refine and prepare it for a seamless performance in the grand realms of exploration and modeling. Just as a masterful conductor fine-tunes an orchestra's instruments before a symphony, data preprocessing holds the baton to crafting predictive models that resonate harmoniously.

Unprocessed data, akin to an untuned instrument, can result in models plagued by lackluster predictions, excessive bias, erratic variance, and even deceptive outcomes. Remember the timeless adage, "Garbage in = Garbage Out." Feeding inadequately prepared data into your models inevitably yields compromised results.

The techniques shared below serve as your compass in the journey of data refinement, ensuring that your data is not only well-prepared but finely tuned before it takes center stage in the grand performance of analysis and insight generation.

4.1 Choreographing the Sequence

In the captivating world of data preprocessing in Python, the sequence in which each step unfolds is of paramount importance, much like the choreography in an intricate ballet. The arrangement of these steps may vary based on the unique objectives of your analysis. Typically, this dance commences with a pas de deux an elegant duet involving the exploration of the original data. This pivotal performance serves as a guiding light, illuminating the intricate terrain that lies ahead.

Much like a dancer's graceful movements influence the flow of a choreography, this exploratory act significantly influences the selection and order of preprocessing techniques to be applied. By intimately acquainting yourself with the nuances and intricacies of the initial data, you lay the foundation for a harmonious and effective preprocessing journey.

As you navigate this choreography of data manipulation in Python, each technique represents a well-choreographed step in your preprocessing routine. The subsequent steps are designed to refine the data's rhythm, correct any discordant notes, and enhance its overall harmony. Whether it's handling missing values, normalizing variables, dealing with outliers, or encoding categorical features, the sequencing of these techniques is crucial.

Just as dancers practice tirelessly to master their moves, your approach to sequencing data preprocessing steps requires careful consideration and a deep understanding of how each technique influences the overall performance. Thus, your data's journey from raw to refined echoes the meticulous practice that transforms a novice dancer into a virtuoso, resulting in a harmonious ensemble of insights and models.

4.2 Subset Variables

In the symphony of data preprocessing in Python, there are instances where achieving harmonious insights demands the meticulous removal of certain variables—akin to refining the composition of an ensemble to achieve a harmonious balance. Allow us to illustrate a well-orchestrated sequence for variable subsetting, leveraging the renowned `iris` dataset found within the **datasets** library.

```
import pandas as pd
from sklearn.datasets import load_iris

iris = load_iris()
data = pd.DataFrame(data=iris.data, columns=iris.feature_names)
```

At the onset of our journey, we turn our attention to the `iris` dataset, an ensemble of variables each playing its distinct role. Gazing upon the opulent dataset, we're presented with a snapshot of this dataset in all its multidimensional glory.

```python
remove = ["petal width (cm)"]
data.drop(remove, axis=1, inplace=True)
data.head()
```

```
##    sepal length (cm)  sepal width (cm)  petal length (cm)
## 0                5.1               3.5                1.4
## 1                4.9               3.0                1.4
## 2                4.7               3.2                1.3
## 3                4.6               3.1                1.5
## 4                5.0               3.6                1.4
```

Now, the stage is set for a graceful variable subsetting performance. In this act, we select a subset of the dancers, each variable representing an artist on the stage, contributing to the composition's richness. To execute this sequence, we've chosen to remove the 'petal width (cm)' variable. With precision and finesse, we manipulate the data ensemble, crafting a refined subset. Witness the transformation, where the rhythm of the dataset shifts, aligning with the deliberate removal of the specified variable. This orchestrated move enhances the clarity of our dataset's melody, creating a harmonious composition ready for further exploration and analysis.

In this elegantly choreographed symphony of data preprocessing in Python, every step is a deliberate note, contributing to the overall harmony. The process of variable subsetting showcases the power of precision in refining your data ensemble, ensuring that each variable resonates harmoniously to produce the insights and models that drive your analytical endeavors.

4.3 Imputing Missing Values

In the symphony of data preprocessing in Python, occasionally, it's crucial to inspect the stage for any gaps in the performance—missing values that might disrupt the rhythm of your analysis. Just as a choreographer ensures that every dancer is present and accounted for, data analysts must address missing values to ensure the integrity of their insights. This preparatory step is akin to ensuring that every instrument in an orchestra is ready to play its part in creating a harmonious composition. The `info()` function takes on the role of spotlight, helping to uncover these gaps and initiate the process of handling them effectively. By conducting this initial inspection, analysts are able to identify which variables have missing values, understand the extent of these gaps, and strategize on how to best address them. Just as a choreographer adapts the choreography if a dancer is unable to perform, data analysts must adapt their analysis techniques to accommodate missing values, ensuring that the performance—much like the insights derived from the data—remains as accurate and meaningful as possible.

```python
import pandas as pd
from sklearn.datasets import load_iris

iris = load_iris()
data = pd.DataFrame(data=iris.data,
columns=iris.feature_names)# Assuming 'data' is your DataFrame
data.info()
```

```
## <class 'pandas.core.frame.DataFrame'>
## RangeIndex: 150 entries, 0 to 149
## Data columns (total 4 columns):
##  #   Column             Non-Null Count  Dtype
## ---  ------             --------------  -----
```

```
## 0    sepal length (cm)   150 non-null    float64
## 1    sepal width (cm)    150 non-null    float64
## 2    petal length (cm)   150 non-null    float64
## 3    petal width (cm)    150 non-null    float64
## dtypes: float64(4)
## memory usage: 4.8 KB
```

Alternatively, for a more precise assessment of missing data, analysts can utilize the formula `percentage_missing = (data.isnull().sum().sum() / (data.shape[0] * data.shape[1])) * 100`. This elegant formula calculates the percentage of missing data within the dataset, offering a comprehensive view of the extent to which gaps exist. This percentage is a valuable metric that can be tailored to focus on specific rows or columns, providing insight into which aspects of the data require attention. Similar to a choreographer evaluating the skill level of individual dancers in preparation for a performance, this method assists analysts in pinpointing the areas of their dataset that demand careful handling. Armed with this percentage breakdown, analysts can prioritize their efforts in addressing missing data, making informed decisions on how to proceed with preprocessing and analysis.

However, in scenarios where data replacement takes the center stage, and the data is of numeric nature, the spotlight shifts to Python's libraries like `pandas` for the task of imputations. Just as a choreographer might bring in understudies to seamlessly fill the gaps when a dancer is unable to perform, these libraries provide mechanisms for systematically filling in missing data points. By loading the necessary libraries, analysts can gracefully handle the process of data imputation. This step is crucial for maintaining the rhythm of the analysis, as imputing missing values ensures that subsequent modeling and exploration are based on complete and consistent datasets. Just as the presence of every dancer is essential for a successful performance, complete data allows analysts to derive accurate and meaningful insights from their analyses.

```python
from sklearn.impute import SimpleImputer

# Assuming 'data' is your DataFrame
imputer = SimpleImputer(strategy="mean")
data_imputed = imputer.fit_transform(data)
data_imputed = pd.DataFrame(data_imputed, columns=data.columns)
data.head()
```

##	sepal length (cm)	sepal width (cm)	petal length (cm)	petal width (cm)
## 0	5.1	3.5	1.4	0.2
## 1	4.9	3.0	1.4	0.2
## 2	4.7	3.2	1.3	0.2
## 3	4.6	3.1	1.5	0.2
## 4	5.0	3.6	1.4	0.2

The meticulous dance of data imputation ensures that no missing value goes unnoticed, leaving no gap in the performance. This attention to detail is vividly portrayed in the imputed dataset, where the imputed values seamlessly integrate with the existing data, creating a harmonious composition. This process serves as a testament to the effectiveness of the imputation process in completing the ensemble and preparing the data for further exploration, analysis, and modeling. Just as skilled performers on stage blend seamlessly to create a captivating spectacle, imputed values are meticulously crafted to fit within the context of the dataset. This imputed dataset serves as a foundation for your data analysis, ensuring that your insights are accurate and meaningful.

4.4 Impute Outliers

In the realm of data preprocessing in Python, much like disruptive dancers in a choreographed performance, outliers have the potential to disrupt the harmony of a dataset. These extreme values can distort the overall patterns and relationships within the data, leading to skewed results and inaccurate models. Python offers various libraries and tools to detect and handle outliers, ensuring the integrity of the dataset.

One such library is `scikit-learn`, which provides versatile techniques for identifying and handling outliers. By incorporating `scikit-learn` alongside other Python libraries, you gain access to powerful tools for detecting and addressing outliers. This partnership enhances your ability to fine-tune the dataset's performance, creating a refined and accurate representation poised for more accurate analysis and modeling.

```python
import pandas as pd
from sklearn.ensemble import IsolationForest

# Assuming 'data' is your DataFrame
clf = IsolationForest(contamination=0.1, random_state=42)
outliers = clf.fit_predict(data)
data['outlier'] = outliers
data = data[data['outlier'] != -1]   # Remove outliers
data.drop(columns=['outlier'], inplace=True)   # Remove the temporary 'outlier' column
data.head()
```

```
##      sepal length (cm)  sepal width (cm)  petal length (cm)  petal width (cm)
## 0                  5.1               3.5                1.4               0.2
## 1                  4.9               3.0                1.4               0.2
## 2                  4.7               3.2                1.3               0.2
## 3                  4.6               3.1                1.5               0.2
## 4                  5.0               3.6                1.4               0.2
```

In this example, we use the Isolation Forest algorithm from `scikit-learn` to detect and remove outliers. The `contamination` parameter controls the proportion of outliers expected in the dataset.

As the curtains draw to a close on the preprocessing symphony, the transformative effects of handling outliers are beautifully showcased in the grand finale. This visualization encapsulates the harmonious collaboration between the outlier removal process and the underlying data, portraying a dataset that has been carefully refined to mitigate the disruptive influence of outliers. However, it's important to note that this exquisite performance not only revitalizes the data but also demands meticulous attention to variable type assignment. Ensuring that each variable retains its intended data type is akin to having dancers skillfully adhere to their roles, maintaining the integrity and coherence of the overall performance.

4.5 Normalization and Feature Engineering

As the captivating dance of preprocessing reaches its crescendo in Python, the spotlight shifts to normalization and the art of feature engineering, both of which form the heart of this intricate performance. In this phase, a seasoned performer, the `scikit-learn` library, steps onto the stage, ready to showcase its expertise in transforming and refining the data. Guided by the rhythm of `scikit-learn`, the data undergoes a remarkable metamorphosis, where scales are harmonized, and variables are ingeniously crafted to enhance their predictive potential. Just as an expert choreographer tailors each movement to create a mesmerizing routine, `scikit-learn` crafts a new rendition of the data that is optimized for subsequent modeling endeavors. With `scikit-learn` leading the way, this part of the dance promises to unveil the data's hidden nuances and set the stage for the ultimate modeling performance.

```python
from sklearn.preprocessing import StandardScaler

import pandas as pd
from sklearn.datasets import load_iris
```

```python
iris = load_iris()
data = pd.DataFrame(data=iris.data, columns=iris.feature_names)

scaler = StandardScaler()
data[['sepal length (cm)', 'sepal width (cm)', 'petal length (cm)', 'petal width (cm)']]
= scaler.fit_transform(data[['sepal length (cm)', 'sepal width (cm)', 'petal length
(cm)', 'petal width (cm)']])
data.head()
```

```
##    sepal length (cm)  sepal width (cm)  petal length (cm)  petal width (cm)
## 0          -0.900681          1.019004          -1.340227          -1.315444
## 1          -1.143017         -0.131979          -1.340227          -1.315444
## 2          -1.385353          0.328414          -1.397064          -1.315444
## 3          -1.506521          0.098217          -1.283389          -1.315444
## 4          -1.021849          1.249201          -1.340227          -1.315444
```

In this captivating transformation narrative, normalization and feature engineering elegantly engage in a harmonious duet. The choreography of this delicate performance is gracefully directed by various functions and methods from `scikit-learn`. This library seamlessly integrates techniques such as scaling and centering to align the scales of variables and center their distributions. Additionally, you can consider correlations among features to create a meticulously choreographed transformation.

```python
import pandas as pd
from sklearn.preprocessing import StandardScaler, MinMaxScaler
from sklearn.compose import ColumnTransformer
from sklearn.pipeline import Pipeline

# Assuming 'data' is your DataFrame
scaler = ColumnTransformer(
    transformers=[
        ('std', StandardScaler(), ['sepal length (cm)', 'sepal width (cm)']),
        ('minmax', MinMaxScaler(), ['petal length (cm)'])
    ],
    remainder='passthrough'
)

transformed_data = scaler.fit_transform(data)
column_names = ['sepal length (cm) (std)', 'sepal width (cm) (std)', 'petal length (cm)
(minmax)', 'petal width (cm)']  # Update with your column names
transformed_data_df = pd.DataFrame(transformed_data, columns=column_names)
transformed_data_df.head()
```

```
##    sepal length (cm) (std)  ...  petal width (cm)
## 0                -0.900681  ...         -1.315444
## 1                -1.143017  ...         -1.315444
## 2                -1.385353  ...         -1.315444
## 3                -1.506521  ...         -1.315444
## 4                -1.021849  ...         -1.315444
##
## [5 rows x 4 columns]
```

In this code, the transformed data is stored in the `transformed_data_df` DataFrame, allowing you to print the head of the DataFrame for the reader to see. Make sure to update `column_names` with the appropriate column names used in your dataset. The `print(transformed_data_df.head())` statement will display the first few rows of the transformed data for better understanding. Embrace the splendor of the grand transformation, where the graceful synchronization of normalization and feature engineering takes center stage under the guidance of the revered `scikit-learn` library. As the curtain rises on this tableau, each variable's scale is harmoniously aligned, ensuring that they contribute equally to the performance of the predictive model. The centered distributions and judicious consideration of inter-variable correlations create a cohesive and balanced ensemble. This coordinated effort between normalization and feature engineering elevates the data to a state of optimal readiness, a stunning transformation that serves as a prelude to the remarkable modeling endeavors that lie ahead.

4.6 Data Type Conversions

In the world of data manipulation and analysis, data transformation is akin to the choreography that breathes life into a dance performance. Each step, each movement, contributes to the overall harmony and coherence of the dance. Similarly, data preprocessing holds the key to crafting models that sing—unprocessed data, much like an out-of-tune instrument, can lead to subpar prediction models, high bias, excessive variance, and even misleading outcomes. As the saying goes, "Garbage in = Garbage Out"—feeding inadequate data into your model yields inadequate results.

Data transformation orchestrates the alignment, refinement, and preparation of data, ensuring that it resonates harmoniously with the goals of your analysis or modeling endeavors. Whether it's cleaning out missing values, taming outliers, normalizing features, or adapting data types, each transformation is a deliberate move towards unveiling the true essence of your data. Just as a skilled choreographer guides dancers to tell a compelling story, your expertise in data transformation empowers your data to convey meaningful insights and narratives. With these techniques in your repertoire, you're equipped to take center stage and perform data-driven symphonies that captivate and illuminate.

4.6.1 Numerical/Integer Conversions

When your data assumes a melodic narrative in string form rather than the numeric harmony you seek, the artful application of Python's type conversion functions provides the remedy. This conversion acts as a conductor's baton, orchestrating the transformation of string-based data into the numeric format required for various analyses, calculations, and modeling endeavors. Just as a skilled musician harmonizes their instruments to create a symphony, your adept use of Python's type conversion functions harmonizes your data, allowing it to seamlessly integrate and resonate within the broader analytical composition. This conversion is a subtle yet crucial maneuver that transforms the underlying data structure, making it dance to the tune of your analytical ambitions.

```
x = "1"
print(type(x))
```

```
## <class 'str'>
```

Observe the sight of a number adorned with quotation marks—a clear indicator of a string data type. When faced with such a scenario, fear not, for the conversion process is remarkably straightforward. A simple application of Python's type conversion functions, such as `int()`, `float()`, or `str()`, serves as your conductor's wand, elegantly transforming these strings into their rightful numeric forms. Just as a skilled choreographer guides dancers to transition seamlessly between movements, your adept manipulation of these conversion functions guides the transition of data from strings to numerics, ensuring that the analytical performance flows harmoniously and without disruption.

```
x = int(x)
print(type(x))
```

```
## <class 'int'>
```

Strings no more, the data type now resonates with numerals. Through the magic of conversion functions like `int()`, the transformation is complete. The data that once adorned the attire of a string type has now donned the attire of numerical precision. This conversion not only aligns your data with its appropriate role in the analytical performance but also ensures that calculations and computations proceed seamlessly. Just as a dancer's costume can influence their movement, the right data type empowers your data to glide effortlessly through the intricate steps of statistical analyses, modeling, and visualization, enriching the overall harmonious rhythm of your data-driven endeavors.

4.6.2 Categorical Data Conversion

If your data is reluctant to align with the categorical rhythm, Python offers a remedy through the use of the `astype()` method in pandas. Categorical data types are valuable when working with variables that have a limited and known set of values, such as labels or categories. By employing the `astype()` method, you can gracefully guide your data through a transformation process, converting it from its current data type (e.g., integer or object) into a categorical data type with well-defined categories. This conversion is particularly useful when dealing with data that has nominal or ordinal attributes, such as survey responses or classification labels. Categorical data types not only efficiently store and manage such information but also enhance your analytical capabilities, enabling you to conduct operations, modeling, and visualizations with precision.

```
import pandas as pd
```

```
data = pd.DataFrame({'Category': [1, 2, 3]})
print(data.dtypes)
```

```
## Category     int64
## dtype: object
```

The data, while currently numeric, lacks the categorical flair. Introducing the `astype()` method, complete with custom category labels. When you need to treat numeric data as categorical, especially when it represents distinct groups or levels, the `astype()` method allows you to convert it into categorical data. By specifying custom labels, you impart meaning to each numeric value, which can be especially valuable when working with ordinal data, where the numeric values have a specific order or hierarchy. Through this method, you not only change the data type but also add context to your analysis. Custom labels replace the numeric codes, making your results more interpretable. This conversion empowers you to work with your data more effectively, whether it's for manipulation, visualization, or modeling, while ensuring that the inherent structure and meaning are accurately preserved.

```
data['Category'] = data['Category'].astype('category')
data['Category'] = data['Category'].cat.rename_categories(["First", "Second", "Third"])
print(data.dtypes)
```

```
## Category     category
## dtype: object
```

With custom labels in place, the transformation morphs numeric values into categorical data. This straightforward yet impactful conversion introduces a layer of interpretation to your data. Instead of dealing with raw numeric values, you're now working with categorical levels that convey meaning and context. Categorical data types are particularly useful for nominal or ordinal data, where different values represent distinct categories or levels. By using the `astype()` method along with custom category labels, you bridge the gap between numerical representation and meaningful interpretation. This not only enhances the clarity of your analyses but also facilitates better communication of your findings. Whether you're visualizing data, conducting statistical tests, or building predictive models, having your data in the form of categorical data types enriches your workflow and contributes to more informed decision-making in Python.

4.6.3 String Conversions

When your data prefers to be in the company of character strings, Python offers a solution through the `str()` method provided by pandas. This transformation is your key to unlock the potential of turning various data types into versatile character strings. Whether you're dealing with numeric values, categories, or even dates, the `str()` method persuades them to adopt the form of strings. This conversion is like a magical spell that allows your data to seamlessly fit into character-based analyses, text processing, or any scenario where string manipulation is vital. By using the `str()` method, you ensure your data's flexibility, enabling it to participate in a diverse range of operations and computations.

```
import pandas as pd

x = 1
print(type(x))
```

```
## <class 'int'>
```

The journey from any data type to the realm of strings is remarkably straightforward and accessible. With a simple invocation of the `str()` method in Python, you open the gateway to a world where your data takes on the form of character strings. This transformation holds incredible power, as it enables you to harmoniously blend different types of data into a unified format, facilitating consistent analysis and processing. Whether you're dealing with numeric values, dates, categories, or any other type, the `str()` method gracefully persuades them into the realm of strings, ensuring that they can seamlessly participate in various string-related operations, concatenations, and manipulations. The simplicity of this conversion belies its impact, making it an essential tool in your arsenal for data preprocessing and transformation tasks.

```
x = str(x)
print(type(x))
```

```
## <class 'str'>
```

4.6.4 Date Conversions

Handling dates in Python's data landscape is akin to guiding enigmatic dancers through a choreographed routine. The intricacies of dates necessitate careful handling to ensure accurate analyses and meaningful insights. Enter Python's datetime library—an instrumental toolkit that facilitates the transformation of various date representations into a standardized format. Whether your dates are presented as strings, numeric values, or other formats, Python's datetime functions adeptly interpret and convert them into a native datetime format. This conversion opens the door to a myriad of possibilities, including chronological analyses, time-based visualizations, and temporal comparisons. By harnessing the capabilities of Python's datetime library, you imbue your data with a coherent temporal structure, enabling you to uncover patterns, trends, and relationships that might otherwise remain hidden in the intricate dance of time.

```python
x = "01-11-2018"
print(type(x))
```

```
## <class 'str'>
```

In the realm of data, dates often present themselves as intricate puzzles that require deciphering and proper formatting. This is where Python's datetime library emerges as a valuable ally. With its ability to transform diverse date representations into a uniform and comprehensible format, Python's datetime functions act as a bridge between the complex world of date data and the structured realm of Python. Whether your dates are stored as strings, numbers, or other formats, applying Python's datetime functions empowers you to unlock the true essence of temporal information. By harmonizing your dates through this transformation, you not only ensure consistent analyses but also set the stage for insightful explorations into time-based patterns, trends, and relationships within your data. Just as a skilled dancer interprets the nuances of music to convey emotion, Python's datetime functions interpret the nuances of date representations to unveil the underlying stories hidden within your data.

```python
from datetime import datetime

x = "01-11-2018"
x = datetime.strptime(x, "%m-%d-%Y")
print(type(x))
```

```
## <class 'datetime.datetime'>
```

4.7   Balancing Data

In the symphony of data analysis, balance holds a significant role, particularly when it comes to factor variables that take center stage as target variables in classification tasks. Achieving balanced data ensures that each class receives equal attention and avoids skewing the predictive model's performance. This is where Python's imbalanced-learn library steps in as a skilled maestro, offering an automated approach to data balancing. With its capabilities, imbalanced-learn orchestrates a harmonious performance by redistributing instances within classes, ultimately resulting in a dataset that better reflects the true distribution of the target variable. This balanced dataset lays the foundation for more accurate model training and evaluation, minimizing the risk of bias and enabling your predictive models to resonate with improved precision across all classes. Just as a skilled conductor fine-tunes each instrument in an orchestra to create a harmonious composition, imbalanced-learn orchestrates the balancing act that is essential for producing reliable and equitable classification models.

```python
from sklearn.datasets import load_iris
from imblearn.over_sampling import RandomOverSampler
import pandas as pd
import numpy as np

# Load the Iris dataset
iris = load_iris()
X = iris.data
y = iris.target

# Initialize RandomOverSampler
ros = RandomOverSampler(random_state=0)
```

24

```python
# Resample the dataset
X_resampled, y_resampled = ros.fit_resample(X, y)

# Check the class distribution after oversampling
unique, counts = np.unique(y_resampled, return_counts=True)
print(dict(zip(unique, counts)))

# Convert resampled data to a DataFrame (optional)
```

```
## {0: 50, 1: 50, 2: 50}
```

```python
resampled_data = pd.DataFrame(data=X_resampled, columns=iris.feature_names)
resampled_data['target'] = y_resampled

# Print the first few rows of the resampled data
print(resampled_data.head())
```

```
##    sepal length (cm)  sepal width (cm)  ...  petal width (cm)  target
## 0                5.1               3.5  ...               0.2       0
## 1                4.9               3.0  ...               0.2       0
## 2                4.7               3.2  ...               0.2       0
## 3                4.6               3.1  ...               0.2       0
## 4                5.0               3.6  ...               0.2       0
##
## [5 rows x 5 columns]
```

Before the harmonious symphony of data balancing begins, it's essential to select the target variable that will be the focus of this intricate performance. Once your target variable is identified, it's wise to ensure it's in the appropriate format for the balancing act. If the target variable is not already balanced, consider transforming it into one. Balancing the target variable allows imbalanced-learn to work its magic effectively, as it can understand the class structure and distribution of the data. This transformation might involve assigning labels or levels to the different classes within the target variable, ensuring that the library comprehends the distinct categories that your model aims to predict. By laying this foundational groundwork, you prepare the stage for imbalanced-learn to guide the data balancing process with finesse and precision, resulting in a more equitable and reliable foundation for model training and evaluation.

```python
from sklearn.preprocessing import LabelEncoder

# Assuming 'y' is your target variable
le = LabelEncoder()
y_encoded = le.fit_transform(y)
print(y_encoded)
```

```
## [0 0 0 0 0 0 0 0 0 0 0 0 0 0 0 0 0 0 0 0 0 0 0 0 0 0 0 0 0 0 0 0 0 0 0 0
##  0 0 0 0 0 0 0 0 0 0 0 0 0 1 1 1 1 1 1 1 1 1 1 1 1 1 1 1 1 1 1 1 1 1 1 1
##  1 1 1 1 1 1 1 1 1 1 1 1 1 1 1 1 1 1 1 2 2 2 2 2 2 2 2 2 2
##  2 2 2 2 2 2 2 2 2 2 2 2 2 2 2 2 2 2 2 2 2 2 2 2 2 2 2 2 2
##  2 2]
```

Observe the captivating transformation unveiled in your resampled dataset. It's a testament to the prowess of imbalanced-learn in orchestrating a harmonious dance of data balancing. The RandomOverSampler from this library takes the stage with finesse, meticulously aligning the representation of features and classes. Through its sophisticated algorithms, imbalanced-learn ensures that each class within the target variable enjoys equitable prominence, setting the scene for more accurate and unbiased model training. Moreover, this library extends its performance to address label noise in classification challenges, catering to the intricacies of real-world data where mislabeled instances can disrupt the rhythm of analysis. As you continue your analysis with this balanced ensemble, it's evident that imbalanced-learn adds a layer of sophistication and reliability to your data preparation endeavors, enriching your modeling outcomes and enabling you to extract meaningful insights from your data-driven performances.

4.8 Advanced Data Processing

In the realm of advanced data processing, two pivotal techniques come to the fore: Feature Selection and Feature Engineering, each wielding its own unique set of strategies to enhance the quality and predictive power of your models. These techniques serve as transformative tools that can elevate your data analysis and modeling endeavors to new heights. By skillfully navigating the landscape of feature selection and engineering, you can effectively curate your dataset to amplify the signal while reducing noise.

Feature Selection, the first aspect, involves the strategic pruning of your dataset to retain only the most influential and informative variables. This process is akin to refining a masterpiece by highlighting the most essential elements. By selecting the right subset of features, you not only streamline the modeling process but also mitigate the risk of overfitting and enhance model interpretability. Importantly, feature selection is not just a manual endeavor; it can also be accomplished through machine learning modeling, which evaluates the predictive power of each feature and retains only those that contribute significantly to the model's performance. We will delve deeper into this technique as we explore regression and classification problems, where machine learning models come to the forefront.

Moving forward, Feature Engineering complements Feature Selection by transforming the existing variables and generating new ones, thus enriching the dataset with a diverse range of information. It's akin to crafting new dance moves that infuse your performance with novelty and depth. Feature engineering empowers you to derive insights from the data that might not be immediately apparent, ultimately enhancing the model's ability to capture complex relationships and patterns. Techniques such as creating interaction terms, polynomial features, and aggregating data across dimensions are just a few examples of how feature engineering can breathe life into your dataset and elevate your modeling accuracy.

While this exploration provides a glimpse into the foundational concepts of feature selection and engineering, our journey will delve further into the intricacies of these techniques in the upcoming sections. By understanding the art of choosing the right features and engineering new ones, you'll be equipped to wield these advanced data processing tools to sculpt your data into a masterpiece that resonates with insights, accuracy, and predictive power.

4.8.1 Feature Selection

Within the pages of this book, we embark on a journey to unveil the intricate world of feature selection, a critical step in the data modeling process that wields the power to refine and optimize your predictive models. Our exploration will encompass two fundamental options for feature selection: Correlation and Variable Importance. These techniques serve as invaluable compasses, guiding you towards the most relevant and impactful features while eliminating noise and redundancy.

The first option, **Correlation**, involves assessing the relationship between individual features and the target variable, as well as among themselves. By quantifying the strength and direction of these relationships, you gain insights into which features are closely aligned with the outcome you aim to predict. Features with strong correlations can provide significant predictive power, while those with weak correlations might be candidates for removal to simplify the model. This approach empowers you to streamline your dataset, ensuring that only the most relevant features contribute to the model's accuracy.

The second option, **Variable Importance**, draws inspiration from the world of machine learning models. It evaluates the impact of individual features on the model's performance, allowing you to distinguish the features that play a pivotal role in making accurate predictions. This method provides a strategic framework for feature selection by leveraging the predictive capabilities of machine learning algorithms. By prioritizing features based on their importance, you can optimize your model's efficiency and effectiveness.

As we embark on this journey, we'll also acknowledge an empirical method that, while comprehensive, may not always be the most practical due to its intensive computational demands. Instead, we'll focus on equipping you with the tools to make informed decisions about feature selection based on correlations and variable importance. The Classical Machine Learning Modeling section will delve deeper into when and how to effectively integrate these techniques into your modeling efforts, ensuring that your models are equipped with the most influential features to achieve accurate and insightful predictions.

4.8.1.1 Correlation Feature Selection   When it comes to feature selection, a practical and effective strategy revolves around the identification and elimination of highly correlated variables. This technique aims to tackle multicollinearity, a scenario in which two or more variables in your dataset are closely interconnected. Multicollinearity can introduce redundancy into your model and potentially create challenges in terms of interpretability, model stability, and generalization.

To employ this approach in Python, you can analyze the correlation matrix of your features and target variable. Variables with correlation coefficients surpassing a predefined threshold are categorized as highly correlated. Typically, a threshold of 0.90 is considered indicative of strong correlation. In some instances, a correlation exceeding 0.95 might even signify singularity, denoting an exceptionally elevated correlation level where the variables offer almost identical information. Upon identifying such notable correlations, you can consider removing one of the variables without compromising critical information. This step not only simplifies your model but also helps alleviate the potential issues tied to multicollinearity.

When addressing a pair of highly correlated variables, the conventional approach is to exclude one of them. However, it's crucial to approach this decision thoughtfully. At times, you might choose to eliminate one variable, assess the model's performance, and then proceed with the other variable. This iterative strategy permits you to gauge the influence of each variable on the model's accuracy. By adhering to these principles and leveraging insights from correlation analysis, you can systematically enhance your dataset, thus elevating the quality and effectiveness of your predictive models.

```python
import pandas as pd
from sklearn.datasets import load_iris

# Load the Iris dataset as an example
iris = load_iris()
data = pd.DataFrame(data=iris.data, columns=iris.feature_names)

# Calculate the correlation matrix
cor = data.corr()
print(cor)
```

```
##                     sepal length (cm)  ...  petal width (cm)
## sepal length (cm)            1.000000  ...          0.817941
## sepal width (cm)            -0.117570  ...         -0.366126
## petal length (cm)            0.871754  ...          0.962865
## petal width (cm)             0.817941  ...          1.000000
##
## [4 rows x 4 columns]
```

In Python, you can utilize libraries like NumPy and pandas to calculate and analyze the correlation matrix of your dataset, as shown in the code example above. This matrix will provide you with insights into the relationships between your features, helping you identify and address highly correlated variables.

4.8.1.2 Variable Importance Feature Selection

Uncovering the true importance of variables in your dataset requires a dynamic process in Python, similar to R. To achieve this, it's necessary to construct a machine learning model, feed it with your data, and then harness the trained model to extract importance measures for each feature. This technique offers a tangible way to quantify the impact of individual variables on the model's predictions. However, the approach you adopt can vary depending on whether you're dealing with a regression or classification problem.

In the realm of feature importance, the choice of model is pivotal in Python, as it is in R. For regression tasks, algorithms like linear regression or decision trees can be suitable choices. On the other hand, for classification problems, models such as random forests or gradient boosting might be more appropriate. The key is to select models that align with the nature of your problem and data, as different models have varying strengths and weaknesses when it comes to estimating feature importance.

As a best practice in Python, it's often wise to go beyond relying on a single model, just as in R. By training multiple models and evaluating the importance of features across them, you gain a more comprehensive and robust understanding of the variables' significance. This comparative approach enables you to identify features that consistently exhibit high importance across various models, making your feature selection decisions more robust and adaptable. In the ever-evolving landscape of data science, this holistic exploration of feature importance equips you with insights that pave the way for effective model building and accurate predictions.

4.8.1.2.1 Variable Importance for Classification Problems

In the pursuit of understanding variable importance for classification problems, we must engage in the realm of modeling. The journey involves constructing and training various classifiers, including the Decision Tree, Random Forest, and Support Vector Machine (SVM), all orchestrated through Python's robust `scikit-learn` library.

Each of these models is trained using the `scikit-learn` framework, with the specific goal of extracting variable importance measures. This measure serves as a guide, directing us towards the most influential variables within the dataset.

What distinguishes this methodology is the use of multiple models. Employing different modeling techniques allows us to generalize the results of variable importance. This holistic approach ensures that the insights gained aren't confined to the peculiarities of a single model, offering a more robust understanding of which variables truly matter. The beauty of this measure lies in its simplicity of interpretation, typically graded on a scale from 0 to 100, where a score of 100 signifies the utmost importance, while 0 denotes insignificance.

As you embark on this journey, ensure you have the `scikit-learn` library installed and be prepared to work with a dataset. For this illustration, we'll use the famous Iris dataset available in `scikit-learn`.

```python
import numpy as np
from sklearn import datasets

# Load the Iris dataset
iris = datasets.load_iris()
X = iris.data
y = iris.target
```

As we delve deeper into the process, a critical step is establishing control parameters that define the terrain of our training endeavors. Configuring the training space often involves techniques like k-fold cross-validation, which provides a comprehensive understanding of the model's generalization capabilities and performance across different samples.

```
from sklearn.model_selection import train_test_split

# Split the dataset into training and testing sets
X_train, X_test, y_train, y_test = train_test_split(X, y, test_size=0.2, random_state=42)
X_train = pd.DataFrame(X_train, columns=iris.feature_names)
X_train.head()
```

```
##    sepal length (cm)  sepal width (cm)  petal length (cm)  petal width (cm)
## 0                4.6               3.6                1.0               0.2
## 1                5.7               4.4                1.5               0.4
## 2                6.7               3.1                4.4               1.4
## 3                4.8               3.4                1.6               0.2
## 4                4.4               3.2                1.3               0.2
```

With our control parameters in place, we can proceed to train the selected model techniques. These models are trained for supervised classification tasks using the `fit()` function.

```
from sklearn.tree import DecisionTreeClassifier
from sklearn.ensemble import RandomForestClassifier
from sklearn.svm import SVC
from sklearn.naive_bayes import GaussianNB

# Create and train the models
decision_tree = DecisionTreeClassifier()
random_forest = RandomForestClassifier()

decision_tree.fit(X_train, y_train)
```

```
## DecisionTreeClassifier()
```

```
random_forest.fit(X_train, y_train)
```

```
## RandomForestClassifier()
```

After successfully training our models, the stored state contains variable importance measures that provide insights into the significance of different features in predicting the target variable.

```
# Extract variable importance scores
decision_tree_importance = decision_tree.feature_importances_
random_forest_importance = random_forest.feature_importances_
```

This observation paves the way for informed decision-making when it comes to feature selection. However, the best practice is to exercise caution and avoid jumping to conclusions based solely on one model's results. The beauty of having trained multiple models lies in the opportunity to compare and contrast the variable importance results across models, enhancing the robustness of your decisions.

```
# Visualize variable importance for Decision Tree
import matplotlib.pyplot as plt
```

```python
# Get feature importances from the trained Decision Tree model
feature_importances = decision_tree.feature_importances_

# Get feature names
feature_names = X_train.columns

# Sort feature importances in descending order
indices = feature_importances.argsort()[::-1]

# Rearrange feature names so they match the sorted feature importances
sorted_feature_names = [feature_names[i] for i in indices]

# Plot the feature importances
plt.figure(figsize=(10, 6))
plt.bar(range(X_train.shape[1]), feature_importances[indices])
#plt.xticks(range(X_train.shape[1]), sorted_feature_names, rotation=90)
```

```
## <BarContainer object of 4 artists>
```

```python
plt.xlabel('Feature')
plt.ylabel('Feature Importance')
plt.title('Variable Importance - Decision Tree')
plt.tight_layout()
plt.show(block=False);
```

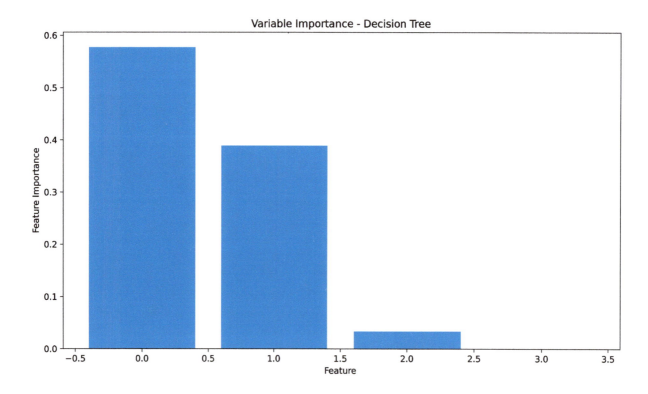

In summary, through the symphony of modeling and feature importance results conducted on the Iris dataset, we can confidently draw conclusions about the variables that are most likely to yield optimal results in our modeling efforts. Armed with this knowledge, we can create a refined subset of the dataset that includes only these pivotal variables, streamlining our efforts and maximizing the potential for accurate predictions in Python.

4.8.1.2.2 Variable Importance for Regression The process of capturing variable importance and selecting significant features for regression problems shares resemblances with the approach we've discussed for classification tasks. In this section, we will delve into the realm of regression by building and training three distinct regression models: the Linear Model, Random Forest, and Support Vector Machine (SVM). Each of these models will be developed using the powerful `scikit-learn` library, which simplifies the process of creating, training, and evaluating machine learning models in Python.

Before embarking on this journey, it's important to import the necessary libraries, including `scikit-learn`. This package will be our guiding companion as we navigate the intricacies of variable importance and model training. By leveraging the standardized workflow provided by `scikit-learn`, we can efficiently build and assess our regression models, ensuring that we capture the most pertinent variables for predictive accuracy.

```python
import numpy as np
import pandas as pd
from sklearn import datasets
from sklearn.model_selection import train_test_split
from sklearn.ensemble import RandomForestRegressor
from sklearn.tree import DecisionTreeRegressor
from sklearn.svm import SVR
from sklearn.linear_model import LinearRegression
from sklearn.metrics import mean_squared_error, r2_score
```

Through this exploration, we aim to determine which variables have the most substantial impact on the regression models' predictive performance. Similar to the classification process, we will employ various techniques to uncover the importance of each feature. However, it's important to note that the evaluation metrics and methodologies may differ slightly due to the distinct nature of regression tasks. The knowledge gained from these variable importance assessments will empower us to select a refined subset of features that hold the greatest potential for yielding accurate and robust regression models.

```python
import yfinance as yf
import pandas as pd
import datetime

# Define the start and end dates for the data
start = datetime.datetime.now() - datetime.timedelta(days=365*5)
end = datetime.datetime.now()

# Fetch historical stock data for GOOG from Yahoo Finance
data = yf.download('GOOG', start=start, end=end)

# Extract the 'Close' prices as the target variable (y)

## [**********************100%%**********************]  1 of 1 completed

y = data['Close']

# Extract features (X), you can choose different columns as features based on your
analysis
X = data[['Open', 'High', 'Low', 'Volume']]
```

31

In our journey of exploring regression models, we will start by splitting our dataset into training and testing sets to assess model performance.

```
X_train, X_test, y_train, y_test = train_test_split(X, y, test_size=0.2, random_state=42)
```

With our data prepared, we can now create and train our regression models. The following code demonstrates how to train a Linear Regression, Random Forest, and Decision Tree regressor using `scikit-learn`.

```
# Create and train the models
linear_model = LinearRegression()
random_forest_model = RandomForestRegressor()
decision_tree_model = DecisionTreeRegressor()

linear_model.fit(X_train, y_train)
```

```
## LinearRegression()
```

```
random_forest_model.fit(X_train, y_train)
```

```
## RandomForestRegressor()
```

```
decision_tree_model.fit(X_train, y_train)
```

```
## DecisionTreeRegressor()
```

After successfully training our models, the next step is to evaluate them using appropriate regression metrics like Mean Squared Error (MSE) and R-squared (R^2).

```
# Make predictions
linear_predictions = linear_model.predict(X_test)
random_forest_predictions = random_forest_model.predict(X_test)
decision_tree_predictions = decision_tree_model.predict(X_test)

# Evaluate model performance
linear_mse = mean_squared_error(y_test, linear_predictions)
random_forest_mse = mean_squared_error(y_test, random_forest_predictions)
decision_tree_mse = mean_squared_error(y_test, decision_tree_predictions)

linear_r2 = r2_score(y_test, linear_predictions)
random_forest_r2 = r2_score(y_test, random_forest_predictions)
decision_tree_r2 = r2_score(y_test, decision_tree_predictions)

print(f'Linear Regression - MSE: {linear_mse}, R^2: {linear_r2}')
```

```
## Linear Regression - MSE: 0.40167808034499203, R^2: 0.9995211652942317
```

```
print(f'Random Forest Regression - MSE: {random_forest_mse}, R^2: {random_forest_r2}')
```

```
## Random Forest Regression - MSE: 0.7516753901413354, R^2: 0.99910393849731
```

```python
print(f'Decision Tree Regression - MSE: {decision_tree_mse}, R^2: {decision_tree_r2}')
```

```
## Decision Tree Regression - MSE: 1.2169327017603906, R^2: 0.9985493118975108
```

With our regression models now trained and evaluated, we can delve into the realm of variable importance examination. By accessing the meta-data of our models, we can uncover the significance of each regressor in influencing the outcome. Specifically, in the linear model we constructed, a quick glance at the variable importance metrics reveals that the SMA variable stands out as remarkably significant, holding a prominent position in influencing the predictions. This insight is crucial for honing in on the essential features that truly drive the predictive power of the model, guiding us toward more focused and informed decision-making in the model refinement process.

```python
# Access feature importances for the Random Forest model
feature_importances = random_forest_model.feature_importances_

# Create a DataFrame to visualize feature importances
importance_df = pd.DataFrame({'Feature': X.columns, 'Importance': feature_importances})
importance_df = importance_df.sort_values(by='Importance', ascending=False)

# Visualize variable importance
import matplotlib.pyplot as plt
plt.figure(figsize=(10, 6))
plt.bar(importance_df['Feature'], importance_df['Importance'])
#plt.xticks(rotation=90)
```

```
## <BarContainer object of 4 artists>
```

```python
plt.title('Variable Importance - Random Forest')
plt.xlabel('Feature')
plt.ylabel('Importance')
plt.show(block=False);
```

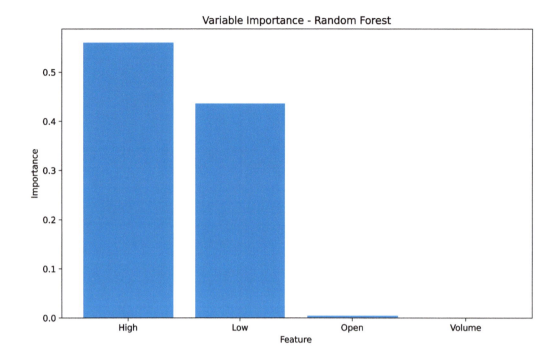

Variable Importance - Random Forest

The insight provided by the decision tree regression model further accentuates the prominence of the `SMA` variable as a crucial determinant in predicting the Close Price of the DEXJPUS. Additionally, the model highlights a potential importance of the `SMA.1` variable, albeit to a lesser degree. This revelation opens up an intriguing avenue for exploration—considering both the `SMA` and `SMA.1` variables in the training of the models. This nuanced perspective prompts us to delve deeper into the potential interplay between these variables and their combined impact on predicting the target variable. By acknowledging the insights from each regression technique, we can make informed decisions about which variables to include, exclude, or further investigate in the modeling process, enhancing our ability to develop accurate predictive models.

It's worth highlighting that among the three regression models utilized, the linear model notably stood out by providing plausible and realistic variable importance measures. The random forest and decision tree models, on the other hand, presented relatively lower values in terms of variable importance. This discrepancy in variable importance measures could be attributed to the nature of these techniques. Random forest and decision tree models, while capable of handling both regression and classification problems, tend to excel more in classification tasks. Their inherent structure, which involves creating splits based on feature importance, might contribute to their relatively diminished sensitivity in discerning variable importance nuances in regression settings.

The variance in the performance of these models underscores the importance of selecting the appropriate modeling technique based on the problem at

hand. While certain techniques might excel in certain scenarios, others might lag behind. This further emphasizes the significance of understanding the strengths and limitations of each modeling approach, enabling practitioners to make informed choices in their data analysis journey. As we venture deeper into the realm of classical machine learning in subsequent chapters, we will delve into these intricacies, shedding light on when and how to harness the full potential of different modeling techniques for both regression and classification problems.

4.8.2 Feature Engineering

In the domain of data manipulation, we encounter a set of techniques known as dimensionality reduction, which fall under the umbrella of unsupervised modeling methods. These techniques play a crucial role in shaping and engineering data, facilitating the transformation of datasets into reduced dimensions. By employing these techniques, we can effectively address problems associated with excessive variables, commonly referred to as dimensions, and transform them into a more manageable set. Despite the reduction in dimensions, these techniques retain crucial information from the eliminated variables, owing to their ability to reconfigure the underlying data structure. Within this context, we will delve into three fundamental techniques: Principal Components Analysis (PCA), Factor Analysis (FA), and Linear Discriminant Analysis (LDA).

Principal Components Analysis (PCA) offers an elegant solution for dimensionality reduction while maintaining interpretability and minimizing information loss. It operates by generating new, uncorrelated variables that systematically maximize variance. By creating these principal components, PCA enables us to condense complex datasets into more easily comprehensible forms, all while retaining the essence of the original data.

Factor Analysis (FA), on the other hand, serves as a potent tool for reducing the complexity of datasets containing variables that are conceptually challenging to measure directly. By distilling a multitude of variables into a smaller number of underlying factors, Factor Analysis transforms intricate data into actionable insights. This process enhances our understanding of the inherent relationships among variables, allowing us to grasp the latent structures that shape the data.

Linear Discriminant Analysis (LDA) takes a distinct approach by focusing on data separation. It seeks to uncover linear combinations of variables that effectively differentiate between classes of objects or events. In essence, LDA aims to decrease dimensionality while preserving the information that distinguishes different classes. By maximizing the separation among classes, LDA enhances the predictive power of the reduced dataset.

In the upcoming sections, we will not only demonstrate the computational aspects of these techniques but also elaborate on their real-world applications. It's crucial to note that their utility extends beyond mere dimensionality reduction; they offer tools for enhanced data exploration, visualization, and, most importantly, improved model performance. As we delve deeper into the chapters on Classical Machine Learning Modeling, we will provide insights into when and how to judiciously employ these techniques to extract meaningful insights from complex datasets in Python.

4.8.2.1 Principal Components Analysis in Python:

While Python's primary strength lies in its diverse libraries and packages for data analysis and machine learning, it provides a convenient way to perform Principal Components Analysis (PCA) through the popular library scikit-learn. Scikit-learn offers a wide range of tools for machine learning and data preprocessing, including PCA.

To utilize PCA in Python with scikit-learn, you can follow these steps:

```python
import pandas as pd
from sklearn.datasets import load_iris
from sklearn.decomposition import PCA
from sklearn.preprocessing import StandardScaler

# Load the iris dataset
data = load_iris()
X = data.data

# Standardize the data (optional but recommended for PCA)
scaler = StandardScaler()
X_scaled = scaler.fit_transform(X)
```

```python
# Apply PCA
pca = PCA()
X_pca = pca.fit_transform(X_scaled)

# Create a DataFrame from the PCA results
pca_df = pd.DataFrame(data=X_pca, columns=[f"PC{i+1}" for i in range(X_pca.shape[1])])

# Concatenate the PCA results with the target variable (if available)
if 'target' in data:
    target = pd.Series(data.target, name='target')
    pca_df = pd.concat([pca_df, target], axis=1)

print(pca_df.head())
```

```
##          PC1       PC2       PC3       PC4  target
## 0 -2.264703  0.480027 -0.127706 -0.024168       0
## 1 -2.080961 -0.674134 -0.234609 -0.103007       0
## 2 -2.364229 -0.341908  0.044201 -0.028377       0
## 3 -2.299384 -0.597395  0.091290  0.065956       0
## 4 -2.389842  0.646835  0.015738  0.035923       0
```

In this Python example, we first load the Iris dataset using scikit-learn, standardize the data (recommended for PCA), apply PCA, and then create a DataFrame to store the PCA results. You can adapt this code to your specific dataset and analysis needs while leveraging the power of scikit-learn for PCA in Python.

4.8.2.2 Factor Analysis Factor analysis in Python can be conducted using the popular library `factor_analyzer`. This library provides tools for performing exploratory and confirmatory factor analysis. Here's a step-by-step guide on how to perform factor analysis using Python:

1. Install the `factor_analyzer` library if you haven't already:

    - `!pip install factor_analyzer`

2. Load the required libraries and your dataset:

```python
import pandas as pd
import numpy as np
from factor_analyzer import FactorAnalyzer
from sklearn.preprocessing import StandardScaler
from sklearn.datasets import load_iris

# Load the iris dataset (or your dataset)
data = load_iris()
X = data.data

# Standardize the data (recommended for factor analysis)
scaler = StandardScaler()
X_scaled = scaler.fit_transform(X)

# Create a DataFrame from the standardized data
df = pd.DataFrame(data=X_scaled, columns=data.feature_names)
```

```
df.head()
# You can also choose specific columns if your dataset is more extensive
# df = df[['column1', 'column2', ...]]
```

```
##     sepal length (cm)  sepal width (cm)  petal length (cm)  petal width (cm)
## 0          -0.900681          1.019004          -1.340227          -1.315444
## 1          -1.143017         -0.131979          -1.340227          -1.315444
## 2          -1.385353          0.328414          -1.397064          -1.315444
## 3          -1.506521          0.098217          -1.283389          -1.315444
## 4          -1.021849          1.249201          -1.340227          -1.315444
```

3. Perform factor analysis using the `FactorAnalyzer` class from `factor_analyzer`:

```
# Initialize the factor analyzer with the desired number of factors (e.g., 1)
n_factors = 1
fa = FactorAnalyzer(n_factors, rotation=None)  # No rotation for simplicity

# Fit the factor analysis model to your data
fa.fit(df)

# Get the factor loadings
```

```
## FactorAnalyzer(n_factors=1, rotation=None, rotation_kwargs={})
```

```
factor_loadings = fa.loadings_

# Transform the data into factor scores
factor_scores = fa.transform(df)
```

4. You can explore the factor loadings and factor scores to gain insights into the relationships between variables and factors:

```
# Print the factor loadings (indicators of variable-factor relationships)
print("Factor Loadings:")
```

```
## Factor Loadings:
```

```
print(pd.DataFrame(factor_loadings, index=df.columns, columns=[f"Factor {i+1}" for i in
range(n_factors)]))

# Print the factor scores (transformed data)
```

```
##                    Factor 1
## sepal length (cm) -0.822986
## sepal width (cm)   0.334364
## petal length (cm) -1.014525
## petal width (cm)  -0.974734
```

```python
print("\nFactor Scores:")
```

```
##
## Factor Scores:
```

```python
print(pd.DataFrame(factor_scores, columns=[f"Factor {i+1}" for i in range(n_factors)]))
```

```
##       Factor 1
## 0     1.369679
## 1     1.622479
## 2     1.414673
## 3     1.163879
## 4     1.202890
## ..         ...
## 145  -0.384656
## 146  -0.289744
## 147  -0.733238
## 148  -1.386371
## 149  -1.227284
##
## [150 rows x 1 columns]
```

Factor analysis in Python provides similar capabilities to the R version, allowing you to uncover underlying structures in your data. By following these steps and using the `factor_analyzer` library, you can conduct factor analysis in Python and gain valuable insights into your dataset.

4.8.2.3 Linear Discriminant Analysis (LDA) in Python:
Performing Linear Discriminant Analysis (LDA) in Python is straightforward using the `scikit-learn` library. LDA is used to find linear combinations of variables that maximize class separation, making it effective for classification tasks. In this example, we will guide you through the process using the classic Iris dataset.

To start, follow these steps to perform LDA in Python:

```python
import pandas as pd
from sklearn.discriminant_analysis import LinearDiscriminantAnalysis
from sklearn.datasets import load_iris

# Load the Iris dataset (or your dataset)
data = load_iris()
X = data.data
y = data.target

# Create a DataFrame from the dataset
df = pd.DataFrame(data=X, columns=data.feature_names)

# Initialize and fit the LDA model
lda = LinearDiscriminantAnalysis()
lda.fit(X, y)

# Transform the data using LDA
```

```
## LinearDiscriminantAnalysis()

new_features = lda.transform(X)

# Convert new_features to a pandas DataFrame
new_df = pd.DataFrame(data=new_features, columns=['LDA1', 'LDA2'])  # Adjust column names
accordingly

# Print the head of the new DataFrame
print(new_df.head())
```

```
##        LDA1       LDA2
## 0  8.061800   0.300421
## 1  7.128688  -0.786660
## 2  7.489828  -0.265384
## 3  6.813201  -0.670631
## 4  8.132309   0.514463
```

Now, you have the transformed dataset stored in the **new_features** array, which contains linear discriminants that maximize class separation. This transformed data can be used for further analysis or classification tasks.

To explore the results of LDA, you can access various attributes of the **lda** object, such as the explained variance ratios and coefficients:

```
# Explained variance ratios of each component
explained_variances = lda.explained_variance_ratio_
print('Explained variance ratios:', explained_variances)

# Coefficients of the linear discriminants
```

```
## Explained variance ratios: [0.9912126 0.0087874]
```

```
coefficients = lda.coef_
print('Coefficients:', coefficients)
```

```
## Coefficients: [[  6.31475846  12.13931718 -16.94642465 -20.77005459]
##  [ -1.53119919  -4.37604348   4.69566531   3.06258539]
##  [ -4.78355927  -7.7632737   12.25075935  17.7074692 ]]
```

These attributes provide valuable insights into the proportion of variance explained by each linear discriminant and the coefficients that indicate the contribution of each original variable to the linear discriminants.

Linear Discriminant Analysis in Python, using **scikit-learn**, offers a powerful feature extraction and dimensionality reduction technique while retaining important information for classification tasks. You can further fine-tune your LDA model by adjusting parameters and exploring the results to meet your specific needs.

4.9 Examples of Processing Data

In the following section, we will guide you through examples of preprocessing data for both regression and classification tasks in the context of machine learning modeling, using Python. While these examples represent only a subset of the available data processing techniques, they illustrate a typical sequence that can be adapted to various types of data and modeling scenarios.

In the realm of machine learning, data preparation is a critical step that significantly impacts the performance and accuracy of your models. The sequence we will cover, encompassing steps like data transformation, feature selection, and dimensionality reduction, provides a structured approach to make your data suitable for various modeling techniques. This preprocessing sequence ensures that your data is appropriately organized, relevant features are chosen, and noise is minimized, ultimately resulting in more precise and dependable models.

It's worth noting that not every modeling problem will necessitate every step in this sequence. However, having a well-defined and organized preprocessing workflow can significantly improve your efficiency and effectiveness when dealing with data for machine learning. By grasping the principles and examples presented in this section, you'll be well-prepared to apply similar strategies to your datasets using Python, tailored to the specific characteristics and requirements of your modeling projects.

4.9.1 Regression Data Processing Example

To illustrate a practical data pre-processing sequence for regression tasks, we'll walk through an example step by step using Python. Our goal is to showcase how different techniques can be applied coherently to prepare data for machine learning tasks. Start by importing the necessary Python libraries for various pre-processing functions.

```python
import pandas as pd
import numpy as np
from sklearn.impute import SimpleImputer
from sklearn.preprocessing import StandardScaler
from sklearn.decomposition import PCA
from sklearn.model_selection import train_test_split
```

For this example, we'll use foreign exchange (forex) data and focus on predicting "Close" prices. Begin by fetching the data using a library like **pandas**. The time series nature of the data makes it suitable for a linear regression problem. After obtaining the data, apply a moving average indicator (SMA) to create additional features that could potentially improve the regression model's performance. Compute SMA indicators with different window sizes (48, 96, and 144) based on the "Close" prices.

```python
import yfinance as yf

# Fetch forex data using Yahoo Finance
start_date = '2018-01-01'
end_date = '2023-01-01'
forex_data = yf.download('GOOG', start=start_date, end=end_date)

# Calculate SMA indicators
```

```
## [**********************100%%**********************]  1 of 1 completed
```

```python
forex_data['SMA_48'] = forex_data['Close'].rolling(window=48).mean()
forex_data['SMA_96'] = forex_data['Close'].rolling(window=96).mean()
forex_data['SMA_144'] = forex_data['Close'].rolling(window=144).mean()

# Drop rows with missing values
```

```
forex_data = forex_data.dropna()

# Reset index
forex_data.reset_index(inplace=True)
```

This code snippet demonstrates how to load data, calculate SMA indicators, handle missing values, and structure the dataset with SMA indicators and "Close" prices.

Next, let's proceed with the pre-processing sequence. We'll start by handling missing values using the `SimpleImputer` from scikit-learn. Then, we'll perform standardization to ensure that all features have the same scale, which is essential for many machine learning algorithms.

```
# Separate features and target variable
X = forex_data[['SMA_48', 'SMA_96', 'SMA_144']]
y = forex_data['Close']

# Handle missing values
imputer = SimpleImputer(strategy='mean')
X_imputed = imputer.fit_transform(X)

# Standardize features
scaler = StandardScaler()
X_standardized = scaler.fit_transform(X_imputed)
```

Now, the data is free from missing values and has been standardized for regression modeling. Last lets impute any outliers.

```
# Outlier detection and imputation
clf = IsolationForest(contamination=0.1, random_state=42)
outliers = clf.fit_predict(X_standardized)
non_outliers_mask = outliers != -1
X_no_outliers = X_standardized[non_outliers_mask]
y_no_outliers = y[non_outliers_mask]


import pandas as pd

# Create a DataFrame with non-outlier features and target variable
non_outliers_df = pd.DataFrame(data=X_no_outliers, columns=['SMA_48', 'SMA_96',
'SMA_144'])
non_outliers_df['Close'] = y_no_outliers
non_outliers_df.head()
# Now, non_outliers_df contains the non-outlier data in a DataFrame format


##       SMA_48    SMA_96    SMA_144        Close
## 0 -1.027817 -1.067066 -1.028853   61.924999
## 1 -1.023113 -1.065700 -1.027118   60.987000
## 2 -1.018161 -1.064565 -1.025608   60.862999
## 3 -1.013451 -1.063386 -1.024110   61.000500
## 4 -1.008520 -1.061871 -1.022722   61.307499
```

Lets perform some feature engineering using PCA.

```
# Standardize features for non-outliers
scaler = StandardScaler()
X_standardized_no_outliers = scaler.fit_transform(non_outliers_df[['SMA_48', 'SMA_96',
'SMA_144']])

# Apply PCA for dimensionality reduction on non-outliers
pca = PCA(n_components=2)   # Choose the number of components
X_pca_no_outliers = pca.fit_transform(X_standardized_no_outliers)

# Create a DataFrame for non-outliers with PCA components and target variable
non_outliers_with_target = pd.DataFrame(data=X_pca_no_outliers, columns=['PCA Component
1', 'PCA Component 2'])
non_outliers_with_target['Target'] = y_no_outliers.values

# Display the combined DataFrame
print("\nCombined DataFrame with PCA Components and Target Variable:")


##
## Combined DataFrame with PCA Components and Target Variable:

print(non_outliers_with_target.head())


##    PCA Component 1  PCA Component 2    Target
## 0        -1.660459        -0.007092  61.924999
## 1        -1.655889        -0.009327  60.987000
## 2        -1.651441        -0.011913  60.862999
## 3        -1.647116        -0.014325  61.000500
## 4        -1.642529        -0.016958  61.307499
```

In summary, this Python-based example showcases a coherent data pre-processing sequence for regression tasks. Starting with data import, feature engineering, and handling missing values, we progress through standardization to prepare the data for regression modeling. This systematic approach enhances the dataset's quality, making it suitable for building accurate regression models.

4.9.2 Classification Data Example

Let's explore a comprehensive sequence of data pre-processing steps through a classification example using Python. This walkthrough will illustrate the importance of each stage and how they collectively contribute to refining the dataset for classification modeling. To begin, we'll load the essential libraries into the Python environment to enable us to execute the required tasks smoothly.

```
import pandas as pd
import numpy as np
from sklearn.impute import SimpleImputer
from sklearn.preprocessing import StandardScaler
from sklearn.decomposition import PCA
from sklearn.utils import resample
```

With the necessary libraries in place, we'll progress through the pre-processing sequence step by step, transforming the raw data into a structured and cleaned dataset ready for classification analysis. This example will help you understand the significance of each pre-processing stage and how they collectively contribute to better data quality and model performance.

For this classification example, we'll use the well-known Iris dataset from the `sklearn.datasets` package. Let's import and examine the data to understand its structure.

```python
from sklearn.datasets import load_iris

# Load the Iris dataset
data = load_iris()
df = pd.DataFrame(data.data, columns=data.feature_names)
df['target'] = data.target

# Display the structure of the dataset
print(df.head())
```

```
##    sepal length (cm)  sepal width (cm)  ...  petal width (cm)  target
## 0                5.1               3.5  ...               0.2       0
## 1                4.9               3.0  ...               0.2       0
## 2                4.7               3.2  ...               0.2       0
## 3                4.6               3.1  ...               0.2       0
## 4                5.0               3.6  ...               0.2       0
##
## [5 rows x 5 columns]
```

In a classification task, identifying the target variable is crucial, as it guides our model in predicting different classes or categories. In this case, the "target" variable represents the iris species we aim to predict. Understanding and defining the target variable correctly form the basis for evaluating model performance and making accurate predictions.

Now, let's remove variables that may not significantly contribute to the classification task. Identifying and eliminating such variables improves computational efficiency and model interpretability. In this example, we'll choose to remove the "sepal length (cm)" variable.

```python
# Drop the "sepal length (cm)" variable
df = df.drop(columns=["sepal length (cm)"])

# Display the modified dataset
print(df.head())
```

```
##    sepal width (cm)  petal length (cm)  petal width (cm)  target
## 0               3.5                1.4               0.2       0
## 1               3.0                1.4               0.2       0
## 2               3.2                1.3               0.2       0
## 3               3.1                1.5               0.2       0
## 4               3.6                1.4               0.2       0
```

Next, we'll perform data pre-processing steps. The first step is handling missing values. Missing values can disrupt classification, so we'll use the `SimpleImputer` from scikit-learn to fill in missing values with plausible estimates.

```python
# Separate features and target variable
X = df.drop(columns=["target"])
y = df["target"]

# Handle missing values
imputer = SimpleImputer(strategy='mean')
X_imputed = imputer.fit_transform(X)
# Create a pandas DataFrame with imputed features and target variable
data = pd.DataFrame(X_imputed, columns=X.columns)
data["target"] = y  # Adding the target variable to the DataFrame
data.head()
```

```
##    sepal width (cm)  petal length (cm)  petal width (cm)  target
## 0               3.5                1.4               0.2       0
## 1               3.0                1.4               0.2       0
## 2               3.2                1.3               0.2       0
## 3               3.1                1.5               0.2       0
## 4               3.6                1.4               0.2       0
```

Now that the dataset is free from missing values, we'll address outliers. Outliers can lead to biased classification.

```python
import pandas as pd
from sklearn.ensemble import IsolationForest

# Assuming 'data' is your DataFrame
clf = IsolationForest(contamination=0.1, random_state=42)
outliers = clf.fit_predict(data)
data['outlier'] = outliers
data = data[data['outlier'] != -1]   # Remove outliers
data.drop(columns=['outlier'], inplace=True)   # Remove the temporary 'outlier' column
data.head()
```

```
##    sepal width (cm)  petal length (cm)  petal width (cm)  target
## 0               3.5                1.4               0.2       0
## 1               3.0                1.4               0.2       0
## 2               3.2                1.3               0.2       0
## 3               3.1                1.5               0.2       0
## 4               3.6                1.4               0.2       0
```

Now that outliers have been handled, we'll focus on balancing the dataset. Imbalanced data, where certain classes are significantly more frequent than others, can lead to biased classifications. We'll use the `resample` function from scikit-learn to balance the dataset.

```python
from sklearn.utils import resample

X = data.drop(columns=["target"])
y = data["target"]

# Balance the dataset using resampling
X_balanced, y_balanced = resample(X, y, random_state=42)
```

44

```python
# Display the balanced dataset shape
print("Balanced dataset shape:", X_balanced.shape)
```

```
## Balanced dataset shape: (135, 3)
```

Finally, we'll perform normalization and feature engineering using Principal Component Analysis (PCA) as a feature engineering step. The goal is to transform the dataset so that each variable contributes equally to classification. We'll use the StandardScaler from scikit-learn to normalize the features and then apply PCA for dimensionality reduction.

```python
# Standardize features
scaler = StandardScaler()
X_standardized = scaler.fit_transform(X_balanced)

# Apply PCA for dimensionality reduction
pca = PCA(n_components=2)   # Choose the number of components
X_pca = pca.fit_transform(X_standardized)

# Display the transformed dataset after PCA
print("\nTransformed Dataset after PCA:")
```

```
##
## Transformed Dataset after PCA:
```

```python
print(pd.DataFrame(X_pca, columns=['PCA Component 1', 'PCA Component 2']).head())

# Prepare the dataset for classification
# In this example, we have already removed ignoble variables, handled missing values,
# addressed outliers, balanced the dataset, and applied PCA for dimensionality reduction.

# Further steps such as train-test split, model training, and evaluation are typically
performed
# on the pre-processed dataset in a classification workflow.
```

```
##      PCA Component 1   PCA Component 2
## 0        -1.473472         -0.537581
## 1        -1.501489          0.295990
## 2         2.547625         -1.053760
## 3        -1.230308         -0.386564
## 4        -0.272394          1.217885
```

In summary, this Python-based classification example showcases a sequence of data pre-processing steps. Starting with the import of data and feature selection, we progress through handling missing values, addressing outliers, balancing the dataset, and performing normalization and feature engineering using PCA. Each step contributes to a cleaner, more balanced dataset, setting the stage for accurate and meaningful classification models.

While the sequence presented here is comprehensive, it's adaptable to fit the specific characteristics of your dataset and classification task. Depending on your needs, you may explore additional pre-processing techniques to further enhance your classification model's performance. This example serves as a foundation, guiding you through core pre-processing procedures and providing a framework for feature engineering with PCA.

5 Unveiling Data through Exploration

In the journey of preparing data for modeling, the exploration phase stands as a crucial checkpoint. It's a stage where you delve into the depths of your data to unveil its nuances, patterns, and characteristics. Exploring the data helps in gaining a comprehensive understanding of its distribution, relationships, and potential anomalies. This exploration process should be applied to both the original dataset and the pre-processed data derived from the sequence of techniques we've discussed earlier.

Statistical summaries offer a snapshot of your data's central tendencies, variations, and distribution patterns. Descriptive statistics such as mean, median, standard deviation, and quartiles provide valuable insights into the spread and variability of your variables. This not only informs you about the basic structure of your data but also helps identify potential outliers or skewed distributions that might affect your model's performance.

Visualization analysis, on the other hand, presents an intuitive and visual way to grasp your data's story. Graphs and charts can reveal trends, clusters, relationships, and potential correlations between variables that might not be immediately apparent in numerical summaries. Techniques like scatter plots, histograms, box plots, and correlation matrices are powerful tools to uncover insights from your data's visual representation.

By performing thorough exploratory analysis on both the original dataset and the pre-processed data in Python, you can effectively validate the efficacy of your pre-processing techniques. The insights gained during exploration guide your understanding of the data's inherent characteristics and aid in identifying potential discrepancies introduced during the pre-processing steps. This iterative process ensures that the data you're presenting to your models is coherent, representative, and conducive to producing accurate and reliable predictions.

5.1 Statistical Summaries

Statistical summary techniques play a pivotal role in unraveling the intricacies of your data by condensing complex information into digestible insights. From simple to robust methods, these techniques provide different layers of understanding about the distribution, central tendencies, and variability of your dataset.

At the simplest level, you have the mean and median, both of which offer measures of central tendency. The mean is the average of all data points and is susceptible to outliers that can skew the result. On the other hand, the median represents the middle value when data is sorted and is less influenced by extreme values.

Moving on, the standard deviation provides a measure of how much individual data points deviate from the mean, giving a sense of the data's spread. It's important to note that these basic statistics are sensitive to outliers, which can distort their accuracy.

Robust summary techniques step in to counter the influence of outliers. The interquartile range (IQR) measures the range between the first and third quartiles, effectively identifying the middle 50% of the data. This is especially useful when you want to analyze the central tendency without being overly affected by outliers.

Another robust technique is the median absolute deviation (MAD), which calculates the median of the absolute differences between each data point and the overall median. MAD provides a more stable measure of dispersion compared to the standard deviation when outliers are present.

Incorporating both simple and robust statistical summary techniques in your data exploration equips you with a holistic view of your data's characteristics. These techniques cater to different scenarios and help you gauge the data's normality, spread, and susceptibility to extreme values. By employing a range of summary methods in Python, you can make more informed decisions about the data's behavior and the potential impact of outliers, ultimately paving the way for better data-driven insights and modeling.

5.1.1 Simple Statistical Summary

Exploring your dataset's statistical summary is a fundamental step in understanding the distribution and characteristics of your variables. The code provided offers a simple yet effective way to obtain a comprehensive overview of your data's numerical and date variables, as well as information about factor variables using Python.

When you execute the code, you're utilizing the `describe()` function on the `iris` dataset. This function neatly organizes key statistics for each variable. For numerical and date variables, it displays the minimum, first quartile (25th percentile), median (50th percentile), mean, third quartile (75th percentile), and maximum values. These statistics provide insights into the central tendency, spread, and distribution of your data.

```python
import pandas as pd
from sklearn.datasets import load_iris

# Load the Iris dataset
data = load_iris()
df = pd.DataFrame(data.data, columns=data.feature_names)

# Display the summary statistics
print(df.describe())
```

##	sepal length (cm)	sepal width (cm)	petal length (cm)	petal width (cm)
## count	150.000000	150.000000	150.000000	150.000000
## mean	5.843333	3.057333	3.758000	1.199333
## std	0.828066	0.435866	1.765298	0.762238
## min	4.300000	2.000000	1.000000	0.100000
## 25%	5.100000	2.800000	1.600000	0.300000
## 50%	5.800000	3.000000	4.350000	1.300000
## 75%	6.400000	3.300000	5.100000	1.800000
## max	7.900000	4.400000	6.900000	2.500000

Moreover, for factor variables, the `describe()` function enumerates the count of each class within the factor, giving you a clear idea of the distribution of categorical data. This is particularly valuable for understanding class imbalances or exploring the prevalence of certain categories.

By running this code in Python, you can quickly obtain a concise summary of the dataset's characteristics, making it easier to identify potential issues, trends, or anomalies in your data. This is a vital step in the data exploration process and serves as a foundation for more in-depth analysis and decision-making in subsequent stages of your data science journey.

5.1.2 Robust Statistical Summaries

For robust summary statistics, you can use other Python libraries like `scipy` and `statsmodels`. Here's how you might use `scipy` to compute various statistical properties:

```python
import pandas as pd
import scipy.stats as stats
from sklearn.datasets import load_iris

# Load the Iris dataset
data = load_iris()
```

```python
df = pd.DataFrame(data.data, columns=data.feature_names)

# Basic statistics
basic_stats = df.describe()

# Coefficient of Variation
cv = df.std() / df.mean()

# Kurtosis
kurt = df.kurtosis()

# Skewness
skew = df.skew()

print("Basic Statistics:")
```

Basic Statistics:

```python
print(basic_stats)
```

##	sepal length (cm)	sepal width (cm)	petal length (cm)	petal width (cm)
## count	150.000000	150.000000	150.000000	150.000000
## mean	5.843333	3.057333	3.758000	1.199333
## std	0.828066	0.435866	1.765298	0.762238
## min	4.300000	2.000000	1.000000	0.100000
## 25%	5.100000	2.800000	1.600000	0.300000
## 50%	5.800000	3.000000	4.350000	1.300000
## 75%	6.400000	3.300000	5.100000	1.800000
## max	7.900000	4.400000	6.900000	2.500000

```python
print("\nCoefficient of Variation:")
```

##
Coefficient of Variation:

```python
print(cv)
```

```
## sepal length (cm)    0.141711
## sepal width (cm)     0.142564
## petal length (cm)    0.469744
## petal width (cm)     0.635551
## dtype: float64
```

```python
print("\nKurtosis:")
```

##
Kurtosis:

```
print(kurt)
```

```
## sepal length (cm)   -0.552064
## sepal width (cm)     0.228249
## petal length (cm)   -1.402103
## petal width (cm)    -1.340604
## dtype: float64
```

```
print("\nSkewness:")
```

```
##
## Skewness:
```

```
print(skew)
```

```
## sepal length (cm)    0.314911
## sepal width (cm)     0.318966
## petal length (cm)   -0.274884
## petal width (cm)    -0.102967
## dtype: float64
```

In this example, `basic_stats` contains the common descriptive statistics, `cv` contains the coefficient of variation, `kurt` contains kurtosis, and `skew` contains skewness. Please make sure to install and import the necessary libraries (`pandas` and `scipy.stats`) before running this code.

5.2   Correlation

Exploring correlations within your dataset is a fundamental step in understanding the relationships between numerical variables in Python. The `corr()` function, as showcased in the code snippet, calculates the pairwise correlation coefficients between variables. Correlation quantifies the degree and direction of linear association between two variables. This information is crucial as it helps uncover patterns, dependencies, and potential interactions among variables, which are valuable insights when preparing for further analysis or modeling.

The correlation coefficient, often denoted as "r," ranges between -1 and 1. A positive value signifies a positive linear relationship, meaning that as one variable increases, the other tends to increase as well. On the other hand, a negative value indicates a negative linear relationship, where an increase in one variable is associated with a decrease in the other.

The magnitude of the correlation coefficient indicates the strength of the relationship. A value close to 1 or -1 indicates a strong linear association, while a value close to 0 suggests a weak or negligible relationship. However, it's important to note that correlation doesn't imply causation. Just because two variables are correlated doesn't necessarily mean that changes in one variable cause changes in the other; there might be underlying confounding factors at play.

Exploring correlations is beneficial for several reasons. First, it helps identify variables that might have redundant information. Highly correlated variables might carry similar information, and including both in a model could lead to multicollinearity issues. Secondly, correlations can reveal potential predictive relationships. For example, if you're working on a predictive modeling task, identifying strong correlations between certain input variables and the target variable can guide feature selection and improve model performance.

```python
import pandas as pd
from sklearn.datasets import load_iris
import seaborn as sns

# Load the Iris dataset
data = load_iris()
df = pd.DataFrame(data.data, columns=data.feature_names)
df['target'] = data.target

# Calculate the correlation matrix
cor = df.corr()
print(cor)
```

```
##                    sepal length (cm)  ...     target
## sepal length (cm)           1.000000  ...   0.782561
## sepal width (cm)           -0.117570  ...  -0.426658
## petal length (cm)           0.871754  ...   0.949035
## petal width (cm)            0.817941  ...   0.956547
## target                      0.782561  ...   1.000000
##
## [5 rows x 5 columns]
```

Overall, leveraging the `corr()` function to explore correlations is an essential part of data analysis in Python. It provides a foundation for making informed decisions when choosing variables for modeling, understanding data relationships, and guiding further exploration or hypothesis generation.

5.3 Visualizations

Visualizing data is a crucial step in the data exploration process in Python as it offers a comprehensive and intuitive understanding of the dataset. While statistical summaries provide numerical insights, visualizations enable you to grasp patterns, distributions, and relationships that might not be apparent through numbers alone. By presenting data in graphical formats, you can quickly identify trends, outliers, and potential areas of interest, making data exploration more effective and insightful.

One of the primary benefits of data visualization is its ability to reveal patterns and trends that might otherwise go unnoticed. Scatter plots, line graphs, and histograms can showcase relationships between variables, helping you identify potential correlations, clusters, or anomalies. For instance, a scatter plot can show the correlation between two variables, while a histogram can provide insights into the distribution of a single variable.

Visualizations also aid in identifying outliers or anomalies within the dataset. Box plots, for instance, display the spread and symmetry of data, making it easy to spot extreme values that might impact the analysis. These outliers could be errors in data collection or genuine instances that require further investigation.

Furthermore, data visualization can facilitate the communication of insights to others, whether they are colleagues, stakeholders, or decision-makers. Visual representations are often more accessible than raw data or complex statistics, making it easier to convey findings and support data-driven decisions. Whether you're presenting to a technical or non-technical audience, effective visualizations enhance your ability to convey the story within the data.

Lastly, data visualization allows for hypothesis generation and exploration. By visually examining data, you might identify new research questions or hypotheses that warrant further investigation. For example, a line graph showcasing a sudden spike in website traffic might lead you to explore potential causes, such as a marketing campaign or external event.

In this context, introducing various techniques for visually exploring data, as outlined in your text, provides readers with a toolkit to extract meaningful insights from their datasets using Python. Scatter plots, histograms, bar charts, and more can help analysts uncover the underlying structures and relationships within their data, leading to more informed decision-making and driving deeper exploration.

5.3.1 Correlation Plot

The `seaborn` and `matplotlib` packages in Python offer powerful tools to visually represent correlation matrices, which are derived from the `corr()` function and provide valuable insights into relationships between numerical variables in a dataset. Through these packages, complex correlation information can be presented in a clear and easily interpretable format, aiding data explorers in understanding the interdependencies between different variables.

Correlation matrices can be quite dense and challenging to interpret, especially when dealing with a large number of variables. The `seaborn` and `matplotlib` packages address this challenge by offering various visualization techniques such as color-coded matrices, heatmaps, and clustered matrices. These visualizations use color gradients to represent the strength and direction of correlations, allowing users to quickly identify patterns and relationships.

Color-coded matrices, for instance, use different colors to represent varying levels of correlation, making it easy to identify strong positive, weak positive, strong negative, and weak negative correlations. Heatmaps add an extra layer of clarity by transforming the correlation values into colors, with a gradient indicating the strength and direction of the relationships. Clustered matrices further enhance the understanding by rearranging variables based on their similarity in correlation patterns, revealing underlying structures within the data.

In summary, the `seaborn` and `matplotlib` packages simplify the interpretation of correlation matrices through visual representations that are not only visually appealing but also aid in identifying trends, clusters, and potential areas of further investigation. By offering multiple visualization options, they enable data analysts to choose the most suitable format for their specific dataset and research goals, enhancing the exploratory data analysis process.

```python
import seaborn as sns
import matplotlib.pyplot as plt
import pandas as pd

from sklearn.datasets import load_iris
import seaborn as sns
# Load the Iris dataset
data = load_iris()
df = pd.DataFrame(data.data, columns=data.feature_names)

# Calculate the correlation matrix 'cor'
cor = df.corr()

# Create a correlation plot
plt.figure(figsize=(8, 6))
sns.heatmap(cor, annot=True, cmap='coolwarm', linewidths=0.5)
plt.title('Correlation Plot')
plt.show(block=False);
```

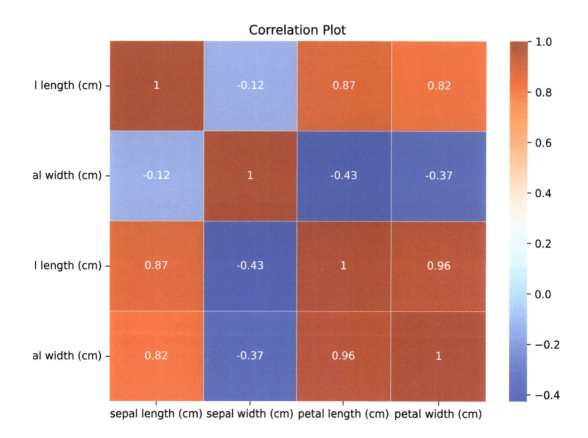

To visualize the interrelationships among variables and assess their degree of correlation, you can refer to the correlation plot above as an illustrative example. This plot offers a comprehensive overview of the correlation coefficients between pairs of variables, allowing you to identify potential patterns and dependencies within the dataset. By examining the color-coded matrix in the correlation plot, you can quickly discern the strength and direction of relationships between variables, enabling you to make informed decisions about which features to include in your modeling process. This visualization serves as a valuable tool to guide feature selection, preprocessing, and ultimately, the development of accurate and effective machine learning models.

5.3.2 Line Plot

When it comes to creating line plots in Python, the `matplotlib` library stands as a versatile and powerful tool for visualization. Developed by John D. Hunter, `matplotlib` offers a highly flexible approach to constructing complex and customized visualizations with ease.

To generate line plots with added features, the `plt.plot()` function within `matplotlib` proves quite useful. This function allows you to plot data and customize the appearance of the lines. By integrating it into your line plot construction, you can easily display meaningful statistics such as means, medians, and more at specific data points along the x-axis.

This functionality is particularly valuable when exploring trends and variations within your dataset. Adding summary statistics to your line plot can provide an insightful glimpse into the central tendencies of your data as well as highlight potential fluctuations or outliers. With the ability to customize the appearance of summary statistics, such as color, size, or style, you can effectively communicate complex information in a straightforward and visually appealing manner.

In conclusion, the `plt.plot()` function within the `matplotlib` library empowers users to create informative line plots that incorporate summary statistics, enriching the visual representation of data trends and variations. This feature enhances the exploration and communication of data patterns, making it a valuable tool in the data analyst's toolkit for effective data visualization and interpretation.

```python
import matplotlib.pyplot as plt
import pandas as pd

# Create a sample DataFrame
data = pd.DataFrame({'Species': ['A', 'B', 'C', 'D', 'E'],
                     'Sepal.Length': [5.1, 4.9, 4.7, 4.6, 5.0]})

# Calculate the mean and standard deviation
mean = data['Sepal.Length'].mean()
std = data['Sepal.Length'].std()

# Create a line plot
plt.figure(figsize=(8, 6))
plt.plot(data['Species'], data['Sepal.Length'], marker='o', linestyle='-')
plt.axhline(y=mean, color='r', linestyle='--', label=f'Mean ({mean:.2f})')
plt.fill_between(data['Species'], mean - std, mean + std, alpha=0.2, label='Mean ± Std Dev')
plt.xlabel('X Variable')
plt.ylabel('Y Variable')
plt.legend()
plt.title('Line Plot with Summary Statistics')
plt.show(block=False);
```

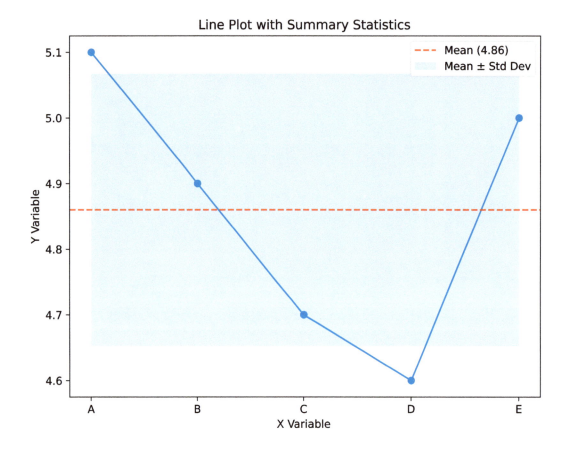

You can find an example of a line plot above. Line charts are particularly effective for illustrating data trends and changes over time. By connecting data points with lines, these plots allow you to easily identify patterns, fluctuations, and shifts in your data. This makes them a valuable tool when analyzing time-series data or any dataset where there's a chronological order to the observations. The x-axis typically represents time, and the y-axis represents the values of the variable you're interested in. Line plots are excellent for conveying the direction and magnitude of changes in your data, making them a staple in exploratory data analysis and data communication.

5.3.3 Bar Plot

Bar plots are an effective visualization tool for displaying categorical data and comparing the frequency or distribution of different categories within a dataset. In Python, you can create versatile barplots using the `matplotlib` library, allowing you to incorporate additional information into the plot.

In a barplot, each category is represented by a bar, and the length of the bar corresponds to the value or count of that category. This makes it easy to make comparisons between categories and quickly identify trends, differences, or similarities. The x-axis typically represents the categories, while the y-axis represents the frequency or value associated with each category.

To summarize data before plotting it in a barplot, you can compute statistics like the mean, median, or count for each category. This can be achieved using Python's data manipulation libraries, such as `pandas`, and then visualizing these summary statistics in the form of bars. This approach not only provides a clear visual representation of the data but also allows for insights into the central tendencies or distributions of different categories.

In this specific instance, the plot displays the average Sepal.Length for each species of iris flowers. The x-axis represents the species, and the y-axis represents the average Sepal.Length. This barplot clearly shows the differences in Sepal.Length across different iris species, making it an effective visualization tool for understanding the variation in this specific attribute.

```python
import matplotlib.pyplot as plt
import pandas as pd

# Create a sample DataFrame
data = pd.DataFrame({'Species': ['setosa', 'versicolor', 'virginica'],
                     'Sepal.Length': [5.1, 5.9, 6.5]})

# Calculate the mean and standard deviation
mean = data['Sepal.Length'].mean()
std = data['Sepal.Length'].std()

# Create a bar plot
plt.figure(figsize=(8, 6))
plt.bar(data['Species'], data['Sepal.Length'], color='lightblue', edgecolor='black',
alpha=0.7)


## <BarContainer object of 3 artists>

plt.axhline(y=mean, color='red', linestyle='--', label=f'Mean ({mean:.2f})')
plt.xlabel('X Variable')
plt.ylabel('Y Variable')
plt.legend()
plt.title('Bar Plot with Summary Statistics')
plt.show(block=False);
```

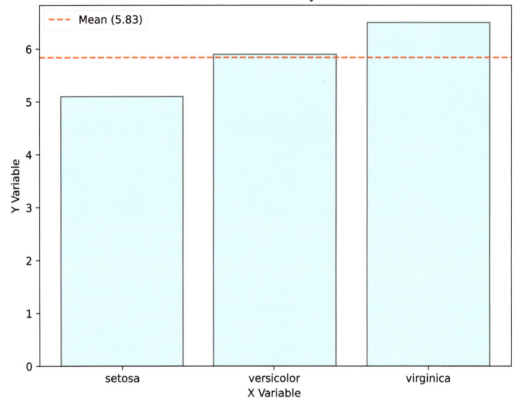

Illustrated above is a representative example of a barplot created using Python's `matplotlib` library. This visualization technique is particularly adept at portraying the distribution and comparison of categorical data or variables. By utilizing bars of varying lengths to represent different categories, this barplot grants a clear understanding of the frequency or counts associated with each category. This intuitive representation aids in identifying trends, patterns, and disparities among categories, empowering data analysts and scientists to derive meaningful insights from their datasets with ease.

5.3.4 Scatter Plot

Scatter plots are invaluable tools in data visualization that allow us to explore the relationship between two numerical variables. In Python, you can create informative scatter plots using the `matplotlib` library, providing flexibility to incorporate additional layers of information.

In a scatter plot, each point represents an observation with specific values for the x-axis and y-axis variables. By visualizing the relationship between these variables, you can gain insights into patterns, trends, correlations, and potential outliers in the data. Scatter plots are particularly useful for identifying relationships between variables, such as linear or nonlinear associations, clusters, or gaps in the data.

The `matplotlib` library offers extensive customization options for scatter plots. You can add layers like trend lines, regression lines, or color-coded groups to provide more context to the plot. This allows for the visualization of trends and patterns that might not be immediately apparent from the raw data. Additionally, you can adjust the appearance of plot elements, including point shape, size, color, and labeling, to enhance the interpretability of the plot.

In this instance, the scatter plot visualizes the relationship between Sepal.Length and Sepal.Width for different species of iris flowers. The x-axis represents Sepal.Length, the y-axis represents Sepal.Width, and each point is color-coded based on the species. This scatter plot offers a clear view of how the two variables are distributed and whether there are any trends or clusters based on the species of the iris flowers.

In summary, scatter plots are versatile and powerful tools for exploring the relationships between numerical variables in your dataset. The flexibility of Python's `matplotlib` library allows you to create visually informative scatter plots that can reveal hidden insights and patterns within your data.

```python
import matplotlib.pyplot as plt
import pandas as pd

# Create a sample DataFrame
data = pd.DataFrame({'Sepal.Length': [5.1, 5.9, 6.5],
                     'Sepal.Width': [3.5, 3.2, 3.0],
                     'Species': ['setosa', 'versicolor', 'virginica']})

# Create a scatter plot with color-coded points
plt.figure(figsize=(8, 6))
plt.scatter(data['Sepal.Width'], data['Sepal.Length'], c=data['Species'].map({'setosa':
'red', 'versicolor': 'green', 'virginica': 'blue'}), label=data['Species'])
plt.xlabel('X Variable')
plt.ylabel('Y Variable')
plt.legend()
plt.title('Scatter Plot with Color-Coded Species')
plt.show(block=False);
```

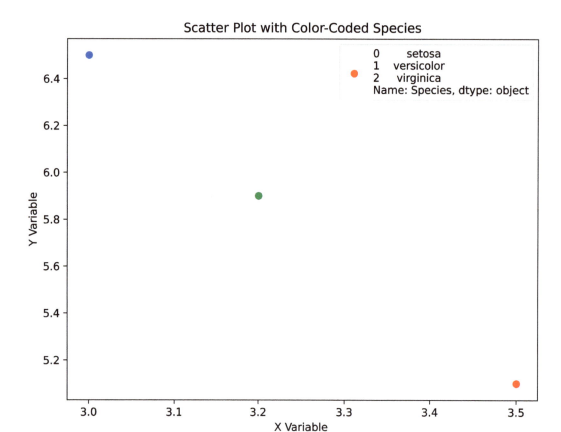

The figure demonstrates how to create a scatter plot using Python's `matplotlib` library. The scatter plot is a valuable visualization technique for understanding relationships between two numerical variables. Using the provided example, you can gain insights into patterns, trends, and correlations within your data.

5.3.5   Histogram Plot

Histograms are essential tools in data visualization that provide insights into the distribution and frequency of numerical data. In Python, you can create informative histograms using the `matplotlib` library, allowing you to understand the underlying patterns and characteristics of a single variable.

A histogram divides the data into intervals, known as bins, and then counts the number of data points that fall into each bin. The resulting plot displays the frequency or count of data points within each bin, creating a visual representation of the data distribution. Histograms are particularly useful for identifying the shape of the data distribution, detecting potential outliers, and understanding the central tendencies and spread of the data.

Using the `matplotlib` library, you can customize histograms to enhance their interpretability and presentation. You can adjust the width of the bins, choose different colors for the bars, and modify the appearance of the axes and labels. By incorporating additional layers like density curves or vertical lines to indicate measures of central tendency, you can provide more insights to the viewer.

The histogram showcases the distribution of Sepal.Length in the iris dataset. Each bar represents the frequency of sepal lengths falling within a specific range. The x-axis represents Sepal.Length, while the y-axis indicates the count of observations within each bin.

In conclusion, histograms are fundamental tools for visualizing the distribution of numerical data, providing a quick and intuitive understanding of the underlying patterns and characteristics. With Python's `matplotlib` library, you can create customized histograms that effectively communicate insights and highlight key aspects of your data distribution.

```python
import matplotlib.pyplot as plt
import pandas as pd

# Create a sample DataFrame
data = pd.DataFrame({'Sepal.Length': [5.1, 5.9, 6.5, 4.8, 5.8, 5.6, 5.7, 5.7, 6.2, 5.1,
5.7],
                     'Species': ['setosa', 'versicolor', 'versicolor', 'setosa',
                     'virginica', 'setosa', 'versicolor', 'virginica', 'setosa',
                     'versicolor', 'virginica']})
x=data['Sepal.Length']
# Create a histogram with customized binwidth and color
plt.figure(figsize=(8, 6))
_ = plt.hist(x, bins=6, color='green', edgecolor='black')
plt.xlabel("X Variable")
```

```
## Text(0.5, 0, 'X Variable')
```

```python
plt.ylabel("Frequency")
```

```
## Text(0, 0.5, 'Frequency')
```

```python
plt.title("Histogram of Sepal.Length")
```

```
## Text(0.5, 1.0, 'Histogram of Sepal.Length')
```

```python
plt.show(block=False);
```

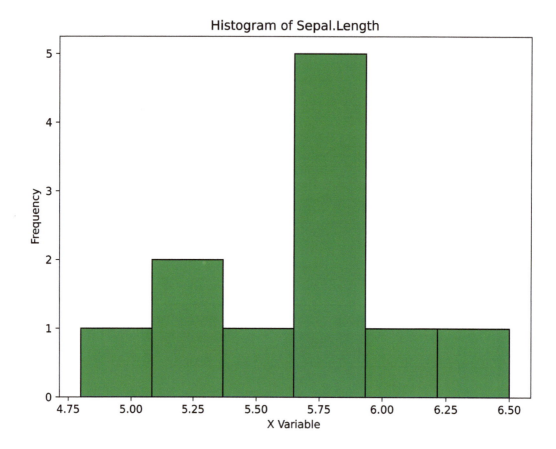

The figure showcases an illustrative instance of a histogram crafted using Python's `matplotlib` library. Histograms are instrumental in comprehending the distribution of a single numerical variable. This visualization aids in identifying patterns, modes, and potential outliers within the data, making it an essential exploratory tool in data analysis.

5.3.6 Box Plot

Box plots, also known as box-and-whisker plots, are valuable tools for visualizing the distribution of data and identifying potential outliers or variations across different categories or groups. These plots are particularly useful when comparing the distribution of a numerical variable within various categories. In a box plot, the data is represented as a box with a central line, known as the median, and "whiskers" extending from the box to show the spread of the data.

In Python, you can create informative box plots using libraries like `matplotlib` and `seaborn`, allowing you to understand the distribution of a numerical variable within different groups.

In a box plot, the box itself represents the interquartile range (IQR), which contains the middle 50% of the data. The line inside the box represents the median, while the "whiskers" extend to show the range of the data within a certain distance from the box. Points outside the whiskers are considered potential outliers.

Creating a box plot involves specifying the response variable (the numerical variable you want to visualize) and the grouping variable (the categorical variable that defines the different groups). The resulting plot will display the distribution of the response variable for each level of the grouping variable.

In summary, box plots are effective tools for comparing the distribution of numerical data across different categories or groups. They enable you to gain insights into the variation of data and identify potential outliers or differences in central tendency among different groups.

```python
import matplotlib.pyplot as plt
import seaborn as sns
import pandas as pd

# Create a sample DataFrame
data = pd.DataFrame({'Sepal.Length': [5.1, 5.9, 6.5, 4.8, 5.8, 5.6, 5.7, 5.7, 6.2, 5.1,
5.7],
                     'Species': ['setosa', 'versicolor', 'versicolor', 'setosa',
                     'virginica', 'setosa', 'versicolor', 'virginica', 'setosa',
                     'versicolor', 'virginica']})

# Create a box plot using seaborn
plt.figure(figsize=(8, 6))
```

```
## <Figure size 800x600 with 0 Axes>
```

```python
sns.boxplot(x='Species', y='Sepal.Length', data=data, palette='Set2')
```

```
## <Axes: xlabel='Species', ylabel='Sepal.Length'>
```

```python
plt.xlabel("Species")
```

```
## Text(0.5, 0, 'Species')
```

```python
plt.ylabel("Sepal Length")
```

```
## Text(0, 0.5, 'Sepal Length')
```

```python
plt.title("Box Plot of Sepal Length by Species")
#plt.xticks(rotation=45)
```

```
## Text(0.5, 1.0, 'Box Plot of Sepal Length by Species')
```

```python
plt.show(block=False);
```

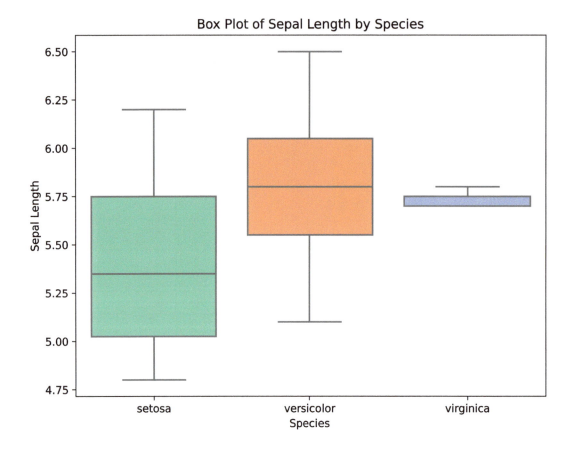

Feel free to consult the figure to observe a representative example of a box plot. Box plots are invaluable for visualizing the distribution, spread, and potential outliers within numerical data across different categories. This visualization technique offers insights into the central tendency and variability of each category, making it particularly useful for making comparisons and identifying patterns in your data.

5.3.7 Density Plot

Density plots, also known as kernel density plots, are valuable tools for visualizing the distribution of data in a continuous numerical variable. They provide a smoothed representation of the data distribution, allowing you to observe patterns that might not be evident in a traditional histogram. Density plots offer a more detailed and continuous view of the data's distribution, making them particularly useful for exploring the shape and characteristics of the data.

In Python, you can create informative density plots using libraries like `matplotlib` and `seaborn`, allowing you to understand the distribution of a continuous numerical variable.

Density plots are particularly useful for identifying modes in the data distribution, understanding the spread of the data, and identifying potential areas of high or low density. By visualizing the density of the data, you can gain a deeper understanding of its underlying distribution, which can be valuable for making informed decisions in data analysis and modeling.

Creating a density plot involves specifying the numerical variable you want to visualize. The resulting plot will show the density distribution of the data. This allows you to assess the shape and characteristics of the data distribution.

In conclusion, density plots are powerful visualization tools for exploring the distribution of continuous numerical data. They enhance your ability to understand the underlying data distribution and identify patterns that might not be apparent in other types of plots. By visualizing the probability density, you can uncover insights about the distribution's shape, spread, and characteristics.

```python
import matplotlib.pyplot as plt
import seaborn as sns
import pandas as pd

# Create a sample DataFrame
data = pd.DataFrame({'Sepal.Length': [5.1, 5.9, 6.5, 4.8, 5.8, 5.6, 5.7, 5.7, 6.2, 5.1,
5.7],
                     'Species': ['setosa', 'versicolor', 'versicolor', 'setosa',
                     'virginica', 'setosa', 'versicolor', 'virginica', 'setosa',
                     'versicolor', 'virginica']})

# Create a density plot using seaborn
plt.figure(figsize=(8, 6))
```

```
## <Figure size 800x600 with 0 Axes>
```

```python
sns.histplot(data['Sepal.Length'], kde=True, color='blue')
```

```
## <Axes: xlabel='Sepal.Length', ylabel='Count'>
```

```python
plt.xlabel("Sepal Length")
```

```
## Text(0.5, 0, 'Sepal Length')
```

```python
plt.ylabel("Density")
```

```
## Text(0, 0.5, 'Density')
```

```python
plt.title("Density Plot of Sepal Length")
```

```
## Text(0.5, 1.0, 'Density Plot of Sepal Length')
```

```python
plt.show(block=False);
```

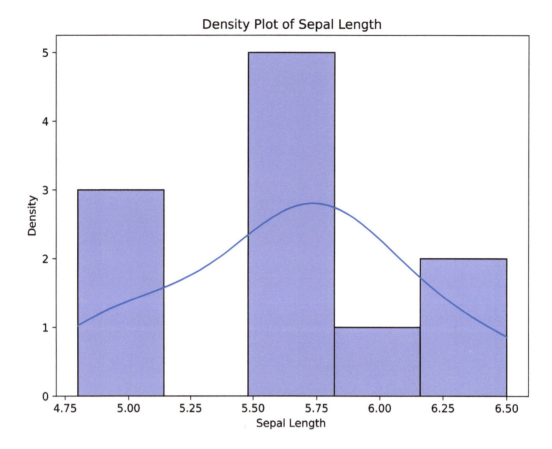

Density plots are effective tools for visualizing the distribution of a single variable's data. They provide a smoothed representation of the underlying data distribution, which can be particularly useful for identifying peaks, gaps, and overall trends in your data. By observing the density plot, you can gain insights into the shape and characteristics of the data distribution, helping you to make informed decisions about modeling and analysis.

5.4 Examples of Data Exploration

Exploring data is a crucial step in the data analysis process, enabling you to understand the characteristics and patterns within your dataset. Let's take a comprehensive look at the steps involved in exploring data using both visual analysis and statistical summaries. We'll consider examples from both regression and classification datasets to provide a well-rounded perspective.

Regression Data Exploration: Imagine you're working with a dataset that contains information about houses, including features such as square footage, the number of bedrooms, and sale prices. Your goal is to predict house prices based on these features. Here's a step-by-step exploration process:

1. **Load and Inspect Data:** Start by loading the dataset and examining its structure using functions like `head()` and `info()` in Python. Understand the variables and their data types.

2. **Statistical Summaries:** Compute basic statistics for numerical variables, such as mean, median, and standard deviation, using the `describe()` function from the `pandas` library. For categorical variables, consider frequency tables.

3. **Correlation Analysis:** Calculate the correlation matrix using the `corr()` function to understand the relationships between numerical variables. Positive, negative, or no correlations can reveal insights into potential predictor variables.

4. **Visual Exploration:** Create scatter plots to visualize relationships between predictor variables and the target variable (house prices). Use libraries like `matplotlib` or `seaborn` to customize the plots and highlight trends or patterns.

   - **Line Plot:** Generate line plots to visualize the relationship between time-related variables (e.g., year built) and house prices. Libraries like `matplotlib` can help you create informative line plots.

   - **Histograms:** Construct histograms to understand the distribution of house prices and other numerical variables. Histograms offer insights into the data's central tendency and spread.

Classification Data Exploration:

Consider a dataset containing information about customer transactions, including features like purchase amount, gender, and age. Your objective is to predict whether a customer will make a repeat purchase. Here's how you can explore this classification dataset:

1. **Load and Inspect Data:** Load the dataset and use functions like `head()` and `info()` to inspect its contents. Identify the variables, data types, and the target variable ("repeat purchase").

2. **Statistical Summaries:** Compute summary statistics for numerical variables using the `describe()` function from the `pandas` library. For categorical variables like gender, calculate frequency tables to understand class distribution.

3. **Visual Exploration:** Create bar plots to visualize the distribution of categorical variables like gender and repeat purchase status. These plots help you understand class proportions and imbalances.

   - **Scatter Plots:** Generate scatter plots to visualize relationships between numerical variables (e.g., purchase amount) and the target variable ("repeat purchase"). This can provide insights into potential predictor variables.

   - **Density Plots:** Utilize libraries like `seaborn` to create density plots. These plots reveal the distribution of numerical variables for different classes (e.g., repeat purchase vs. no repeat purchase).

   - **Box Plots:** Construct box plots using libraries like `seaborn` to compare the distribution of numerical variables across classes. This visual analysis helps identify potential differences in feature distributions.

By following this systematic exploration process, you'll gain a deep understanding of the data, uncover patterns, and identify potential predictor variables for your regression or classification tasks. Exploring data from multiple angles using both statistical summaries and visualizations enhances your ability to make informed decisions throughout the analysis and modeling phases.

5.4.1 Regression Exploration Example

In your quest to become proficient in machine learning with Python, mastering the foundational steps of data exploration and analysis is essential. **Step 1: Importing Essential Libraries**. Begin your journey by importing crucial libraries. **Pandas**, a powerful data manipulation library, simplifies working with structured data. **NumPy** enhances your numerical computing capabilities, enabling complex mathematical operations. **Matplotlib** provides basic plotting functionalities, while **Seaborn** elevates your visualizations with advanced aesthetics.

Step 2: Loading the Dataset. Your adventure begins with loading your dataset into Python. Regardless of the data's source—be it a CSV file, a database, or another format—loading your data is the foundational step. Here's how you can load your dataset:

```
import pandas as pd
import yfinance as yf

# Fetch forex data using Yahoo Finance
start_date = '2018-01-01'
end_date = '2023-01-01'
data = yf.download('GOOG', start=start_date, end=end_date)

# Calculate SMA indicators
```

```
## [*********************100%%**********************]  1 of 1 completed
```

```
data['SMA_48'] = data['Close'].rolling(window=48).mean()
data['SMA_96'] = data['Close'].rolling(window=96).mean()
data['SMA_144'] = data['Close'].rolling(window=144).mean()

# Drop rows with missing values
data = data.dropna()

# Reset index
data.reset_index(inplace=True)
```

Step 3: Understanding the Data. With your data loaded, gain preliminary insights using the `info()` function in Pandas. This function provides an overview of the dataset, including the data types and the presence of non-null values. This understanding is invaluable for shaping your analysis:

```
print(data.info())
```

```
## <class 'pandas.core.frame.DataFrame'>
## RangeIndex: 1116 entries, 0 to 1115
## Data columns (total 10 columns):
##  #   Column     Non-Null Count  Dtype
## ---  ------     --------------  -----
##  0   Date       1116 non-null   datetime64[ns]
##  1   Open       1116 non-null   float64
##  2   High       1116 non-null   float64
##  3   Low        1116 non-null   float64
##  4   Close      1116 non-null   float64
##  5   Adj Close  1116 non-null   float64
##  6   Volume     1116 non-null   int64
##  7   SMA_48     1116 non-null   float64
##  8   SMA_96     1116 non-null   float64
##  9   SMA_144    1116 non-null   float64
## dtypes: datetime64[ns](1), float64(8), int64(1)
## memory usage: 87.3 KB
## None
```

Step 4: Generating a Statistical Summary. Dive deeper into your data by generating a statistical summary. Utilize the `describe()` function to obtain key statistics for numeric columns. This summary, offering metrics like mean, standard deviation, and quartiles, unveils the data's distribution:

```
print(data.describe())
```

```
##                Open          High     ...       SMA_96      SMA_144
## count  1116.000000   1116.000000     ...  1116.000000  1116.000000
## mean     89.885945     90.902891     ...    88.233805    87.086563
## std       31.071245     31.363287     ...    31.113603    30.994881
## min       48.695000     50.176998     ...    53.603375    55.211688
## 25%       60.875001     61.346874     ...    58.360917    57.947785
## 50%       79.675747     80.822502     ...    75.065036    71.306061
## 75%      115.855623   117.423876     ...   116.445151   117.743348
## max      151.863495   152.100006     ...   143.739651   141.481372
##
## [8 rows x 9 columns]
```

Step 5: Exploring Correlations. Explore the relationships between variables using correlation analysis. Compute the correlation matrix and visualize it as a heatmap. This step assists in feature selection and informs your modeling decisions:

```python
import seaborn as sns
import matplotlib.pyplot as plt

correlation_matrix = data.corr()
sns.heatmap(correlation_matrix, annot=True, cmap='coolwarm')
```

```
## <Axes: >
```

```python
plt.title('Correlation Heatmap')
```

```
## Text(0.5, 1.0, 'Correlation Heatmap')
```

```python
plt.show(block=False);
```

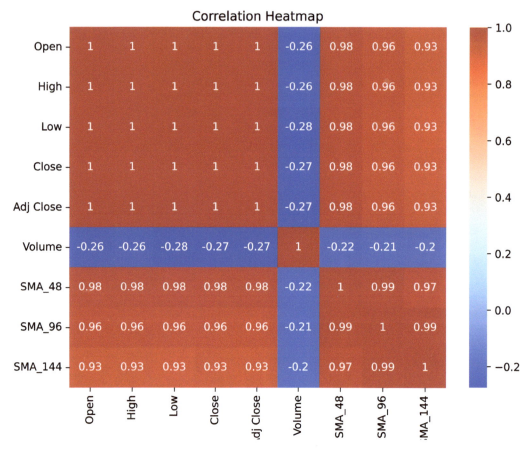

Step 6: Visualizing Complex Relationships. Delve into intricate interconnections with pairplots. These plots offer a comprehensive view of relationships between multiple variables. By combining scatterplots and histograms, pairplots enrich your understanding:

```
sns.pairplot(data)
```

```
## <seaborn.axisgrid.PairGrid object at 0x000000005F90ABC0>
```

```
plt.title('Pairplot')
```

```
## Text(0.5, 1.0, 'Pairplot')
```

```
plt.show(block=False);
```

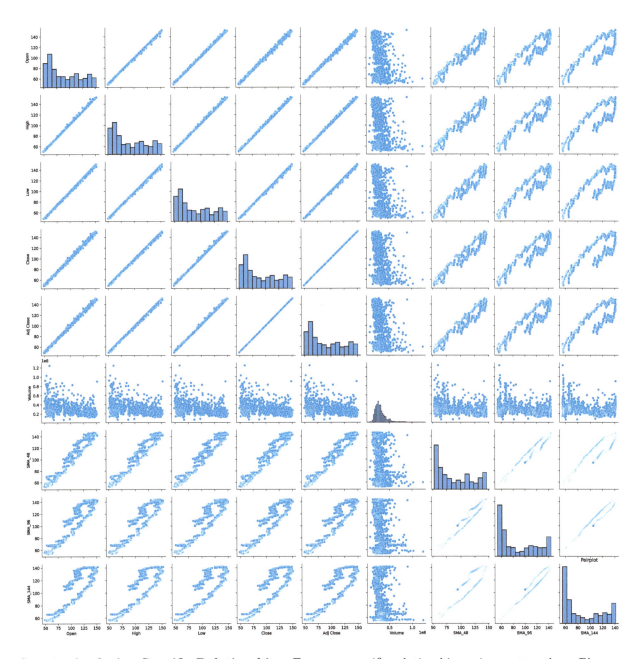

Step 7: Analyzing Specific Relationships. Focus on specific relationships using scatter plots. Plot two selected variables against each other to uncover nuanced patterns and correlations:

```
plt.figure(figsize=(8, 6))
```

```
## <Figure size 800x600 with 0 Axes>
```

```
plt.scatter(data['SMA_96'], data['SMA_144'])
```

```
## <matplotlib.collections.PathCollection object at 0x000000006161EE60>
```

```
plt.xlabel('SMA 96')

## Text(0.5, 0, 'SMA 96')

plt.ylabel('SMA 144')

## Text(0, 0.5, 'SMA 144')

plt.title('Scatter Plot: SMA 96 vs. SMA 144')

## Text(0.5, 1.0, 'Scatter Plot: SMA 96 vs. SMA 144')

plt.show(block=False);
```

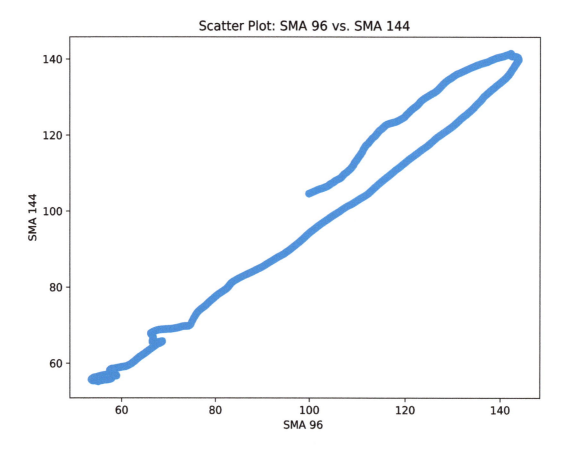

Mastering these steps not only equips you with a solid foundation in data exploration but also sets the stage for advanced machine learning techniques. By combining theory with practical implementation, you transform raw data into actionable insights and intelligent predictions, harnessing the full potential of Python in your data science endeavors. Happy exploring!

5.4.2 Classification Exploration Example

In this section, let's explore a classification dataset extracted from the `datasets` package using Python. First, ensure you have the necessary libraries loaded:

```python
import pandas as pd
import seaborn as sns
import matplotlib.pyplot as plt
from sklearn.datasets import load_iris
```

By importing these libraries, we equip ourselves with tools for effective data exploration and visualization tailored for classification datasets. Let's begin by loading the classification data from the `datasets` package and understanding its structure:

```python
# Load the Iris dataset
data = load_iris()
df = pd.DataFrame(data.data, columns=data.feature_names)
df['target'] = data.target

# Print the structure of the dataset
print(df.info())
```

```
## <class 'pandas.core.frame.DataFrame'>
## RangeIndex: 150 entries, 0 to 149
## Data columns (total 5 columns):
##  #   Column             Non-Null Count  Dtype
## ---  ------             --------------  -----
##  0   sepal length (cm)  150 non-null    float64
##  1   sepal width (cm)   150 non-null    float64
##  2   petal length (cm)  150 non-null    float64
##  3   petal width (cm)   150 non-null    float64
##  4   target             150 non-null    int32
## dtypes: float64(4), int32(1)
## memory usage: 5.4 KB
## None
```

Upon obtaining the dataset, the initial step is to generate a comprehensive statistical summary. This summary provides crucial insights into the dataset's central tendencies, dispersions, and distributional patterns:

```python
# Generate a statistical summary
print(df.describe())
```

```
##        sepal length (cm)  sepal width (cm)  ...  petal width (cm)      target
## count         150.000000        150.000000  ...        150.000000  150.000000
## mean            5.843333          3.057333  ...          1.199333    1.000000
## std             0.828066          0.435866  ...          0.762238    0.819232
## min             4.300000          2.000000  ...          0.100000    0.000000
## 25%             5.100000          2.800000  ...          0.300000    0.000000
## 50%             5.800000          3.000000  ...          1.300000    1.000000
## 75%             6.400000          3.300000  ...          1.800000    2.000000
## max             7.900000          4.400000  ...          2.500000    2.000000
##
## [8 rows x 5 columns]
```

Next, conduct a correlation analysis to ascertain relationships between numeric variables:

```python
# Calculate correlation coefficients
correlation_matrix = df.corr()

# Visualize the correlation matrix
plt.figure(figsize=(8, 6))
```

```
## <Figure size 800x600 with 0 Axes>
```

```python
sns.heatmap(correlation_matrix, annot=True, cmap='coolwarm')
```

```
## <Axes: >
```

```python
plt.title('Correlation Heatmap')
```

```
## Text(0.5, 1.0, 'Correlation Heatmap')
```

```python
plt.show(block=False);
```

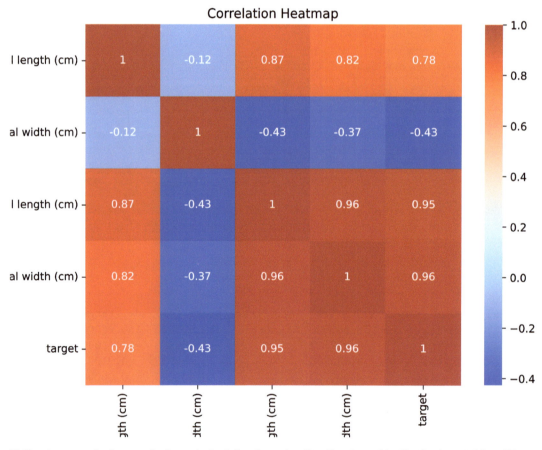

Following correlation analysis, gain insights into the distribution of individual variables. Histogram plots are valuable for visualizing the frequency distribution of numerical variables:

```python
# Plot a histogram for a specific variable
plt.figure(figsize=(8, 6))
```

<Figure size 800x600 with 0 Axes>

```python
sns.histplot(df['sepal width (cm)'], kde=True, color='green')
```

<Axes: xlabel='sepal width (cm)', ylabel='Count'>

```python
plt.xlabel('Sepal Width (cm)')
```

Text(0.5, 0, 'Sepal Width (cm)')

```python
plt.ylabel('Frequency')
```

Text(0, 0.5, 'Frequency')

```python
plt.title('Histogram: Sepal Width')
```

Text(0.5, 1.0, 'Histogram: Sepal Width')

```python
plt.show(block=False);
```

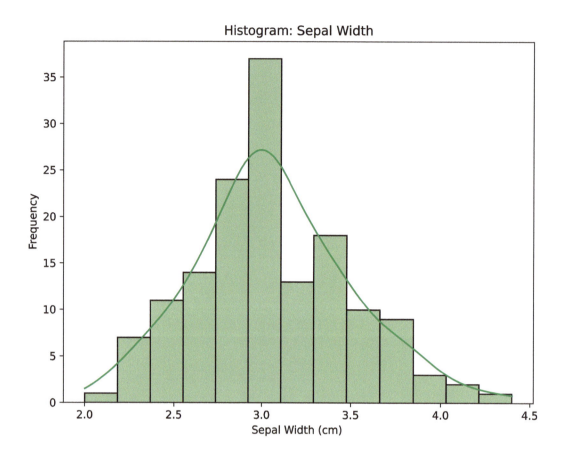

Additionally, understand the density distribution of input variables through density plots:

```
# Plot density plots for input variables
plt.figure(figsize=(12, 8))
```

```
## <Figure size 1200x800 with 0 Axes>
```

```
sns.set(style="whitegrid")
sns.pairplot(df, diag_kind="kde", markers='|', hue='target', plot_kws={'alpha':0.8})
```

```
## <seaborn.axisgrid.PairGrid object at 0x00000000638113F0>
```

```
plt.suptitle('Density Plots for Input Variables', y=1.02)
```

```
## Text(0.5, 1.02, 'Density Plots for Input Variables')
```

```
plt.show(block=False);
```

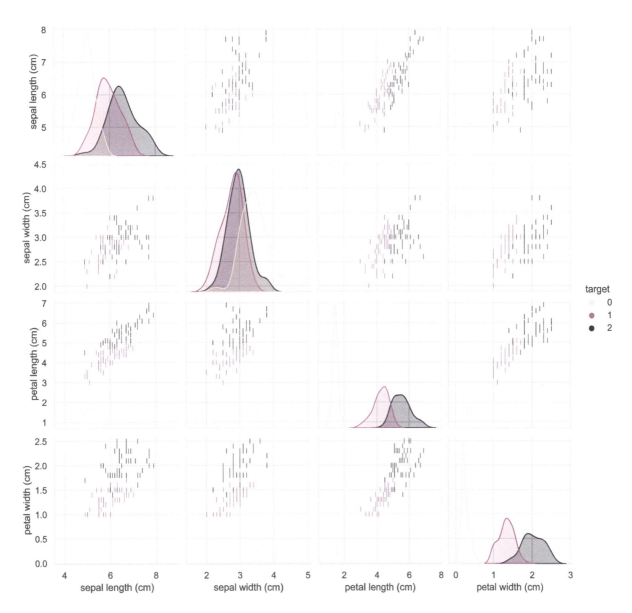

Density plots offer a smooth representation of the data's probability density function, allowing you to observe the concentration of data points across different ranges of values.

By mastering these exploration techniques, you enhance your understanding of the classification dataset. These insights are invaluable for making informed decisions during the preprocessing and modeling stages of machine learning. Happy exploring!

6 Embracing Classical Machine Learning Techniques

When venturing into the realm of machine learning modeling, adopting a structured and systematic approach is paramount to ensuring the success and reliability of your models. We will guide you through our recommended approach for conducting machine learning modeling, encompassing several essential stages.

6.1 Modeling Techniques

In this section, we explore a variety of powerful modeling techniques commonly used in classical machine learning, all implemented in Python. These techniques form the cornerstone of predictive modeling and can be applied to a wide range of regression tasks. Let's delve into each technique's underlying concepts, strengths, and applications, providing you with a comprehensive understanding of their capabilities.

Linear Regression is a fundamental technique used to model the relationship between a dependent variable (target) and one or more independent variables (features). It assumes a linear relationship between the features and the target, aiming to find the best-fitting linear equation that minimizes the difference between predicted and actual values. Linear Regression serves as an excellent starting point for grasping the basic principles of modeling, offering interpretable coefficients that reflect the impact of each feature on the target variable.

Decision Trees offer a more flexible approach by recursively splitting the data based on feature conditions. Each internal node of the tree represents a decision based on a feature, and each leaf node corresponds to a predicted value. Decision Trees are capable of capturing nonlinear relationships and interactions between features. They are easy to visualize and interpret, making them useful for gaining insights into how different features contribute to predictions. However, single decision trees are prone to overfitting and may not generalize well to unseen data.

To address the limitations of individual decision trees, we turn to **Random Forests**. This ensemble technique combines multiple decision trees to improve prediction accuracy and reduce overfitting. Each tree in the forest is trained on a bootstrapped subset of the data, and features are sampled at each split. The final prediction is obtained through a majority vote or averaging of the individual tree predictions. Random Forests are robust, capable of handling high-dimensional data, and can capture complex relationships. They are a versatile choice for a wide range of regression problems.

Support Vector Machines are a versatile family of algorithms that can be used for both classification and regression tasks. In the context of regression, SVMs aim to find a hyperplane that best fits the data while maximizing the margin between the data points and the hyperplane. This results in an effective balance between fitting the data and preventing overfitting. SVMs can capture intricate relationships in the data and perform well even in high-dimensional spaces. However, they may require careful tuning of parameters to achieve optimal performance.

In the upcoming sections, we will dive deeper into each of these techniques, providing hands-on examples and explaining how to implement them using popular libraries in Python.

6.2 Regression Problems

In this section, readers will delve into a variety of techniques specifically designed to tackle regression-type problems using Python. These techniques are indispensable tools in the arsenal of any data scientist or machine learning practitioner, enabling the prediction of numerical values or continuous outcomes.

The techniques we will explore include:

- **Linear Regression (LR):** Foundational and powerful, linear regression assumes a linear relationship between input features and the target variable. It provides a simple yet effective method for modeling relationships between variables and making accurate predictions.

- **Decision Trees (DT):** Decision trees are versatile tools that recursively split data based on features, forming a tree-like structure of decisions. They are easy to understand and interpret, making them invaluable for gaining insights into data relationships.

- **Random Forest (RF):** Random forests, an ensemble technique, construct multiple decision trees and combine their predictions. This ensemble approach reduces overfitting and enhances prediction accuracy. Random forests excel at capturing complex interactions and nonlinear relationships within data.

- **Support Vector Machines (SVM):** Effective for both classification and regression tasks, SVMs aim to find a hyperplane that best fits the data while maximizing the margin between data points and the hyperplane. They are particularly useful in handling high-dimensional data and intricate relationships.

Each technique offers a unique perspective on the data, with its own set of strengths and limitations. Linear Regression provides a straightforward interpretation of relationships, Decision Trees allow for nonlinearity and feature interactions, Random Forests harness the power of ensembles, and Support Vector Machines efficiently handle complex datasets.

By comprehensively understanding and mastering these techniques in Python, you will establish a strong foundation for addressing regression problems. This knowledge will empower you to choose the right technique for specific problems, fine-tune models for optimal performance, and extract meaningful insights from your data.

6.2.1 Linear Regression

In this section, we explore solving a regression problem using a dataset of linear data sourced from the `pandas` and `statsmodels` packages in Python. To start, we import the necessary libraries.

```python
import pandas as pd
import statsmodels.api as sm
from sklearn.model_selection import train_test_split
from sklearn.linear_model import LinearRegression
from sklearn.metrics import mean_squared_error, r2_score
```

Now, let's implement Linear Regression using `sklearn`:

```python
import yfinance as yf

# Fetch forex data using Yahoo Finance
start_date = '2018-01-01'
end_date = '2023-01-01'
data = yf.download('GOOG', start=start_date, end=end_date)
```

```
## [*********************100%%**********************]  1 of 1 completed
```

```python
X = data.drop(columns=['Close'])
y = data['Close']

X_train, X_valid, y_train, y_valid = train_test_split(X, y, test_size=0.3,
random_state=42)
# Initializing the Linear Regression model
lr_model = LinearRegression()
```

Here, an instance of the Linear Regression model is created using `LinearRegression()` from `sklearn.linear_model`. This model will be trained on the training data to learn the underlying patterns in the features and target variable.

```
# Training the model
lr_model.fit(X_train, y_train)
```

LinearRegression()

The `fit` method is called on the model with the training data (`X_train` and `y_train`). This step trains the model by adjusting its parameters based on the input features (`X_train`) and the corresponding target values (`y_train`). During this process, the model learns to map input features to target values.

```
# Making predictions
predictions = lr_model.predict(X_valid)
```

After the model is trained, the `predict` method is used to generate predictions for the test data (`X_test`). The model uses the learned patterns to predict the target values corresponding to the test input features.

```
# Evaluating the model
mse = mean_squared_error(y_valid, predictions)
r2 = r2_score(y_valid, predictions)

print(f'Mean Squared Error: {mse}')
```

Mean Squared Error: 8.807936651640162e-18

```
print(f'R-squared: {r2}')
```

R-squared: 1.0

In these lines, the model's predictions (`predictions`) are compared with the actual target values (`y_test`) to evaluate its performance. Mean Squared Error (MSE) measures the average squared difference between the predicted and actual values, giving an idea of the overall prediction accuracy. R-squared (R2) score represents the proportion of the variance in the target variable that is predictable from the input features. An R2 score closer to 1 indicates a better-fitted model.

Printing these metrics provides insights into how well the model performs on unseen data. Lower MSE and higher R2 values indicate a more accurate and reliable regression model. These metrics are essential for understanding the model's quality and can be used to compare different models or tuning parameters to achieve the best predictive performance.

Python's `sklearn` (scikit-learn) library provides an extensive collection of regression models. Beyond linear regression, `sklearn` offers versatile options such as Support Vector Machines (`SVR`), Decision Trees (`DecisionTreeRegressor`), Random Forests (`RandomForestRegressor`), and many others. Each of these models has distinct strengths and is suitable for various types of data, allowing practitioners to choose the most appropriate method based on the problem at hand and the underlying characteristics of the dataset.

In Chapter @ref(evaluation), we'll delve into a detailed exploration of evaluation metrics like R-squared, Mean Absolute Error (MAE), Mean Squared Error (MSE), and more. These metrics provide a comprehensive understanding of the model's performance, enabling informed decisions about model selection, parameter tuning, and enhancements to improve predictive power.

6.2.2 Decision Tree

In this section, we explore solving a regression problem using a decision tree regressor, an essential machine learning algorithm, in Python. We begin by importing the necessary libraries, including **pandas** for data manipulation and **sklearn.tree** for the decision tree model.

```python
import pandas as pd
from sklearn.model_selection import train_test_split
from sklearn.tree import DecisionTreeRegressor
from sklearn.metrics import mean_squared_error, r2_score
```

Next, we retrieve the data, similar to our previous examples, by fetching the daily price data for the 'GOOG' stock over the past five years.

```python
import yfinance as yf

# Fetch forex data using Yahoo Finance
start_date = '2018-01-01'
end_date = '2023-01-01'
data = yf.download('GOOG', start=start_date, end=end_date)
```

```
## [*********************100%%**********************]  1 of 1 completed
```

We set up the model evaluation parameters, splitting the data into training and testing sets. The **train_test_split** function divides the data into training and testing subsets, with 70% for training and 30% for testing.

```python
X = data.drop(columns=['Close'])
y = data['Close']

X_train, X_test, y_train, y_test = train_test_split(X, y, test_size=0.3, random_state=42)
```

Now, we initialize the decision tree regressor model, train it using the training data, and make predictions on the test data.

```python
# Initializing the Decision Tree Regressor model
model = DecisionTreeRegressor(random_state=42)

# Training the model
model.fit(X_train, y_train)

# Making predictions
```

```
## DecisionTreeRegressor(random_state=42)
```

```python
predictions = model.predict(X_test)
```

To evaluate the model's performance, we calculate Mean Squared Error (MSE) and R-squared (R2) score. MSE measures the average squared difference between predicted and actual values, while R2 score represents the proportion of the variance in the target variable that is predictable from the input features.

```
# Evaluating the model
mse = mean_squared_error(y_test, predictions)
r2 = r2_score(y_test, predictions)

print(f'Mean Squared Error: {mse}')


## Mean Squared Error: 0.05146747700550973

print(f'R-squared: {r2}')


## R-squared: 0.9999462467432413
```

In this approach, we showcase the power of decision tree regression for solving numerical prediction problems. Decision trees are versatile algorithms capable of capturing complex relationships in the data. By understanding how to apply them effectively, you can harness their potential for a wide array of regression tasks. This section demonstrates the flexibility of machine learning techniques and underscores the importance of selecting the right algorithm for each specific problem to achieve accurate and meaningful predictions.

6.2.3 Random Forest

In this section, we delve into solving a regression problem using the random forest algorithm, a robust machine learning technique, in Python. To begin, we import the necessary libraries, including **pandas** for data manipulation and **sklearn.ensemble** for the random forest model.

```
import pandas as pd
from sklearn.model_selection import train_test_split
from sklearn.ensemble import RandomForestRegressor
from sklearn.metrics import r2_score
```

Next, we retrieve our dataset, similar to our previous examples, by fetching the daily price data for the 'GOOG' stock over the past five years.

```
import yfinance as yf

# Fetch forex data using Yahoo Finance
start_date = '2018-01-01'
end_date = '2023-01-01'
data = yf.download('GOOG', start=start_date, end=end_date)


## [*********************100%%**********************]  1 of 1 completed
```

Setting up the model evaluation parameters, we split the data into training and testing sets. The `train_test_split` function divides the data into training and testing subsets, with 70% for training and 30% for testing.

```
X = data.drop(columns=['Close'])
y = data['Close']

X_train, X_test, y_train, y_test = train_test_split(X, y, test_size=0.3, random_state=42)
```

Now, we initialize the random forest regressor model, train it using the training data, and make predictions on the test data.

```python
# Initializing the Random Forest Regressor model
model = RandomForestRegressor(n_estimators=100, random_state=42)

# Training the model
model.fit(X_train, y_train)

# Making predictions
```

```
## RandomForestRegressor(random_state=42)
```

```python
predictions = model.predict(X_test)
```

To evaluate the model's performance, we use the R-squared (R2) score, which measures the proportion of the variance in the target variable that is predictable from the input features.

```python
# Evaluating the model
r2 = r2_score(y_test, predictions)
print(f'R-squared: {r2}')
```

```
## R-squared: 0.9999551914428988
```

In this approach, we showcase the effectiveness of the random forest algorithm for regression tasks. Random forests are powerful ensemble models capable of capturing complex relationships in the data. By employing this technique, you can create accurate predictive models, especially when dealing with datasets containing intricate patterns and multiple variables. This section emphasizes the versatility of machine learning algorithms and highlights the importance of choosing the appropriate model for specific problems to ensure accurate and reliable predictions.

6.2.4 Support Vector Machine

In this section, we'll tackle a regression problem using a sample of linear data similar to our previous approaches, but this time employing a Support Vector Machine (SVM) regressor from the `sklearn` module in Python. To get started, let's import the necessary libraries:

```python
import pandas as pd
from sklearn.model_selection import train_test_split
from sklearn.svm import SVR
from sklearn.metrics import r2_score
```

Now, let's load the data, assuming we have fetched the daily price data for 'GOOG' spanning the last month. We will use a tiny dataset in this case due to the compute necessary for the more modern learning technique:

```python
import yfinance as yf

# Fetch forex data using Yahoo Finance
start_date = '2023-01-01'
end_date = '2023-01-31'
data = yf.download('GOOG', start=start_date, end=end_date)
```

```
## [*********************100%%%**********************]  1 of 1 completed
```

Setting up the model evaluation parameters, we split the data into training and testing sets. The `train_test_split` function divides the data into training and testing subsets, with 70% for training and 30% for testing.

```python
X = data.drop(columns=['Close'])
y = data['Close']

X_train, X_test, y_train, y_test = train_test_split(X, y, test_size=0.3, random_state=42)
```

Next, we set up the parameters for training the SVM model. We'll use 10-fold cross-validation, a common practice in machine learning, and the R-squared metric for evaluation:

```python
# Split the data into training and validation sets
X_train, X_valid, y_train, y_valid = train_test_split(X, y, test_size=0.3,
random_state=42)

# Initialize the SVM regressor
svm_regressor = SVR(kernel='linear')

# Train the model
svm_regressor.fit(X_train, y_train)
```

```
## SVR(kernel='linear')
```

After training the model, it's time to assess its predictability. Use the trained model to make predictions on the validation data and evaluate its performance:

```python
# Generate predictions
predictions = svm_regressor.predict(X_valid)

# Calculate R-squared score
r2 = r2_score(y_valid, predictions)
print(f'R-squared: {r2}')
```

```
## R-squared: -15606084876602.555
```

In this section, we've demonstrated how to apply a Support Vector Machine (SVM) regressor from the `sklearn` module to solve a regression problem. By utilizing this versatile algorithm, you can expand your toolkit for addressing various real-world scenarios. Understanding different machine learning models and their applications equips you with the knowledge to choose the most suitable approach for your specific problem domain.

6.2.5 Compare Trained Regression Models

The following instructions will provide the necessary steps to conduct a comparision of trained machine learning models in-order to determine the best performing model for your use case.

Step 1: Import Necessary Libraries

```python
# Import necessary libraries
from sklearn.linear_model import LinearRegression
from sklearn.tree import DecisionTreeRegressor
from sklearn.ensemble import RandomForestRegressor
from sklearn.svm import SVR
from sklearn.model_selection import cross_val_score
import matplotlib.pyplot as plt
```

In this step, we import the required libraries. We use scikit-learn's `LinearRegression`, `DecisionTreeRegressor`, `RandomForestRegressor`, and `SVR` classes for different regression models. We also import `cross_val_score` for performing cross-validation and `matplotlib.pyplot` for visualization.

Step 2: Initialize Regression Models

```python
# Initialize regression models
lm = LinearRegression()  # Linear Regression model
dt = DecisionTreeRegressor(random_state=42)  # Decision Tree Regressor model with a fixed random state for reproducibility
rf = RandomForestRegressor(random_state=42)  # Random Forest Regressor model with a fixed random state for reproducibility
svm = SVR()  # Support Vector Machine Regressor model
```

Here, we create instances of the Linear Regression, Decision Tree Regressor, Random Forest Regressor, and Linear SVM models. Setting `random_state=42` ensures reproducibility of results.

Step 3: Prepare Data (Assuming X_train and y_train are available)

```python
import yfinance as yf

# Fetch forex data using Yahoo Finance
start_date = '2023-01-01'
end_date = '2023-01-31'
data = yf.download('GOOG', start=start_date, end=end_date)
```

```
## [*********************100%%***********************]  1 of 1 completed
```

```python
X = data.drop(columns=['Close'])
y = data['Close']

X_train, X_test, y_train, y_test = train_test_split(X, y, test_size=0.3, random_state=42)
```

Ensure you have your training features (`X_train`) and target values (`y_train`) ready for model training.

Step 4: Perform Cross-Validation

```python
# Perform cross-validation for each model
lm_scores = cross_val_score(lm, X_train, y_train, cv=5, scoring='r2')  # Cross-validation for Linear Regression
dt_scores = cross_val_score(dt, X_train, y_train, cv=5, scoring='r2')  # Cross-validation for Decision Tree Regressor
rf_scores = cross_val_score(rf, X_train, y_train, cv=5, scoring='r2')  # Cross-validation for Random Forest Regressor
svm_scores = cross_val_score(svm, X_train, y_train, cv=5, scoring='r2')  # Cross-validation for Linear SVM
```

We use `cross_val_score` to perform 5-fold cross-validation for each regression model. `cv=5` specifies 5 folds, and `scoring='r2'` indicates that we're using R-squared as the evaluation metric.

Step 5: Store Results in a Dictionary

```python
# Store the results in a dictionary
results = {'Linear Regression': lm_scores,
           'Decision Tree': dt_scores,
           'Random Forest': rf_scores,
           'Linear SVM': svm_scores}
```

We store the cross-validation scores for each model in a dictionary for easy access and comparison.

Step 6: Create a Dot Plot for Visualization

```python
# Create a dot plot for visualization
plt.figure(figsize=(8, 6))
```

```
## <Figure size 800x600 with 0 Axes>
```

```python
_ = plt.boxplot(list(results.values()), labels=list(results.keys()))
plt.ylabel('R-squared')  # Label for the y-axis indicating R-squared values
```

```
## Text(0, 0.5, 'R-squared')
```

```python
plt.title('Comparison of Trained Regression Models')  # Title of the plot
```

```
## Text(0.5, 1.0, 'Comparison of Trained Regression Models')
```

```python
plt.show(block=False);  # Display the dot plot
```

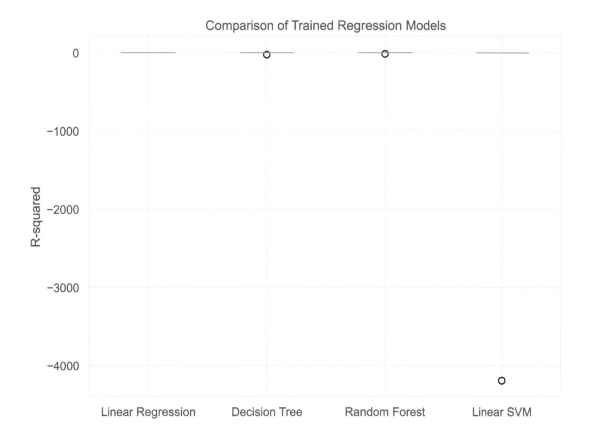

In this step, we create a dot plot using `matplotlib`. The boxplot visually represents the R-squared scores of each regression model, making it easier to compare their performance. The y-axis represents R-squared values, and the x-axis shows the models' names. The dot plot provides a clear and concise comparison of the trained regression models.

By following these steps, you can effectively compare the performance of different regression models using cross-validation and visualize the results using a dot plot, aiding in the selection of the most suitable model for your regression problem.

6.2.6 Regression Example

In this section, we will explore a comprehensive regression example using Python, demonstrating a systematic approach from data preprocessing to model evaluation. Python offers a rich ecosystem of libraries, making it an ideal choice for this task. Let's start by importing the necessary libraries essential for our analysis. This example will showcase the practical implementation of these techniques in a real-world scenario, providing valuable insights into their effectiveness and application.

```
import pandas as pd
import numpy as np
from sklearn.model_selection import train_test_split
from sklearn.impute import SimpleImputer
from sklearn.ensemble import IsolationForest
from sklearn.preprocessing import StandardScaler
from sklearn.metrics import mean_squared_error
```

```python
from sklearn.tree import DecisionTreeRegressor
from sklearn.ensemble import RandomForestRegressor
import yfinance as yf
```

We will use the same dataset as in the previous regression example. To load the data and perform initial preprocessing steps, execute the following code:

```python
# Fetch forex data using Yahoo Finance
start_date = '2022-01-01'
end_date = '2023-01-01'
data = yf.download('GOOG', start=start_date, end=end_date)
```

```
## [**********************100%%**********************]  1 of 1 completed
```

```python
target = data['Close']
# Remove unnecessary variables
dataset = data.drop(columns=['Volume'])
dataset = data.drop(columns=['Close'])

# Check for missing values and handle them
#print(dataset.isnull().sum())
imputer = SimpleImputer(strategy='mean')
dataset_imputed = pd.DataFrame(imputer.fit_transform(dataset), columns=dataset.columns)

# Standardize features
scaler = StandardScaler()
dataset_standardized = scaler.fit_transform(dataset_imputed)

# Detect and remove outliers
clf = IsolationForest(contamination=0.1, random_state=42)
outliers = clf.fit_predict(dataset_standardized)

non_outliers_mask = outliers != -1
dataset_no_outliers = dataset_imputed[non_outliers_mask].reset_index(drop=True)
```

After these preprocessing steps, the data is cleansed, missing values are imputed, and outliers are removed. The features are also standardized for modeling. Next, split the dataset into training and validation sets (80/20 split ratio) to train and evaluate the regression models:

```python
# Assuming 'target' is your target variable
X = dataset_no_outliers
y = target[non_outliers_mask]  # Ensure target corresponds to non-outlier data points

X_train, X_valid, y_train, y_valid = train_test_split(X, y, test_size=0.2,
random_state=42)
```

Define and train a decision tree regression model:

```python
dt_regressor = DecisionTreeRegressor(random_state=42)
dt_regressor.fit(X_train, y_train)

# Predict on the validation set
```

```
## DecisionTreeRegressor(random_state=42)

dt_predictions = dt_regressor.predict(X_valid)

# Calculate RMSE for decision tree model
dt_rmse = np.sqrt(mean_squared_error(y_valid, dt_predictions))
print("Decision Tree RMSE:", dt_rmse)


## Decision Tree RMSE: 0.6675714866143211
```

Define and train a random forest regression model:

```
rf_regressor = RandomForestRegressor(random_state=42)
rf_regressor.fit(X_train, y_train)

# Predict on the validation set


## RandomForestRegressor(random_state=42)

rf_predictions = rf_regressor.predict(X_valid)

# Calculate RMSE for random forest model
rf_rmse = np.sqrt(mean_squared_error(y_valid, rf_predictions))
print("Random Forest RMSE:", rf_rmse)


## Random Forest RMSE: 0.5241800166664446
```

In this example, we used a decision tree regressor and a random forest regressor to model the data. We calculated the Root Mean Squared Error (RMSE) on the validation set to evaluate the models' performance. RMSE provides a measure of how well the models are predicting the target variable, with lower values indicating better performance.

By following this systematic approach, from data preprocessing to model training and evaluation, you can effectively tackle regression problems using machine learning techniques in Python. Each step is essential for ensuring the quality and reliability of your regression models, leading to more accurate predictions in real-world applications.

6.3   Classification Problems

When it comes to solving classification problems, where the goal is to assign data points to predefined categories, several powerful techniques are at your disposal. Each of these techniques has its strengths and unique characteristics, making them suitable for different types of classification tasks. In this section, we'll delve into the core concepts of five essential classification techniques: Logistic Regression, Decision Trees, Random Forests, Support Vector Machines (SVM), and Naive Bayes.

Logistic Regression is a foundational classification technique that models the probability of a data point belonging to a particular class. It's particularly useful when dealing with binary classification problems, where the target variable has two possible outcomes. Logistic Regression employs a logistic (sigmoid) function to transform a linear combination of features into a probability score. This technique provides interpretable coefficients that offer insights into how each feature contributes to the classification decision.

Decision Trees extend their utility to classification tasks as well. In this context, they create a tree-like structure where internal nodes represent feature-based decisions, and leaf nodes correspond to class labels. Decision Trees excel at capturing nonlinear relationships and interactions between features. They are intuitive to understand and visualize, making them valuable tools for uncovering decision paths within your data. However, individual Decision Trees may suffer from overfitting, which can be addressed by ensemble techniques like Random Forests.

When aiming for improved classification accuracy and enhanced robustness, **Random Forests** come to the forefront. This ensemble technique aggregates the predictions of multiple Decision Trees, trained on different subsets of the data. By introducing randomness in feature selection and bootstrapping, Random Forests mitigate overfitting and generalize well to unseen data. They're suitable for handling high-dimensional feature spaces and can capture complex relationships in the data. Random Forests are a versatile choice for a broad range of classification problems.

Support Vector Machines (SVM) are another classification workhorse that strives to find an optimal hyperplane to separate different classes while maximizing the margin between them. SVMs are well-suited for scenarios where the classes are not linearly separable. They can use various kernel functions to transform the feature space into higher dimensions, allowing them to capture intricate decision boundaries. SVMs offer flexibility and robustness, although they may require careful parameter tuning to achieve optimal performance.

Naive Bayes is a probabilistic classification technique based on Bayes' theorem and the assumption of feature independence given the class label. Despite its simplicity, Naive Bayes often performs surprisingly well, especially when dealing with text classification and other high-dimensional problems. It's efficient, requires relatively small amounts of training data, and can handle categorical and continuous features. Naive Bayes is particularly useful for cases where computational efficiency is essential.

In the following sections, we will take a deep dive into each of these classification techniques. We'll provide hands-on examples using python and explain how to implement these techniques using popular libraries. You'll learn how to prepare your data, train the models, evaluate their performance, and fine-tune their parameters. By the end of this book, you'll have a solid understanding of these essential classification techniques and be well-equipped to apply them to real-world classification challenges.

6.3.1 Logistic Regression

In this section, we will explore a classification problem using the `LogisticRegression` class from the `sklearn.linear_model` module in Python. Let's begin by importing the necessary packages:

```
from sklearn.model_selection import train_test_split
from sklearn.linear_model import LogisticRegression
from sklearn.metrics import accuracy_score, precision_score, recall_score, f1_score,
confusion_matrix
from sklearn.datasets import load_iris
```

Next, load the *'iris'* dataset, a commonly used multi-class dataset for classification tasks:

```
iris = load_iris()
X = iris.data
y = iris.target
```

Split the data into training and validation sets:

```python
X_train, X_valid, y_train, y_valid = train_test_split(X, y, test_size=0.3,
random_state=7)
```

Create and train the logistic regression model:

```python
lr_model = LogisticRegression(random_state=7)
lr_model.fit(X_train, y_train)
```

```
## LogisticRegression(random_state=7)
```

Make predictions on the validation data and calculate classification metrics:

```python
predictions = lr_model.predict(X_valid)
accuracy = accuracy_score(y_valid, predictions)
precision = precision_score(y_valid, predictions, average='weighted')
recall = recall_score(y_valid, predictions, average='weighted')
f1 = f1_score(y_valid, predictions, average='weighted')

# Print the metrics
print("Accuracy: {:.2f}".format(accuracy))
```

```
## Accuracy: 0.91
```

```python
print("Precision: {:.2f}".format(precision))
```

```
## Precision: 0.91
```

```python
print("Recall: {:.2f}".format(recall))
```

```
## Recall: 0.91
```

```python
print("F1 Score: {:.2f}".format(f1))

# Confusion Matrix
```

```
## F1 Score: 0.91
```

```python
conf_matrix = confusion_matrix(y_valid, predictions)
print("Confusion Matrix:")
```

```
## Confusion Matrix:
```

```python
print(conf_matrix)
```

```
## [[12  0  0]
##  [ 0 14  2]
##  [ 0  2 15]]
```

In conclusion, logistic regression is a valuable tool for classification problems. By utilizing the `LogisticRegression` class, we demonstrated effective data preprocessing, model training, and evaluation using various classification metrics. Logistic regression provides a versatile approach for modeling binary and multi-class classification scenarios, enabling informed predictions and insights from data. This foundational knowledge will pave the way for exploring more advanced machine learning techniques in the future.

6.3.2 Random Forest

In this section, we will explore solving a classification problem using a robust Random Forest model in Python. To begin, import the necessary packages:

```python
from sklearn.model_selection import train_test_split
from sklearn.ensemble import RandomForestClassifier
from sklearn.metrics import accuracy_score, precision_score, recall_score, f1_score,
confusion_matrix
from sklearn.datasets import load_iris
```

Next, load the dataset from the `load_iris` function in the `sklearn.datasets` module, providing us with the 'iris' dataset:

```python
iris = load_iris()
X = iris.data
y = iris.target
```

Now, split the data into training and validation sets using the `train_test_split` function:

```python
X_train, X_valid, y_train, y_valid = train_test_split(X, y, test_size=0.3,
random_state=7)
```

Create and train the Random Forest model:

```python
rf_model = RandomForestClassifier(random_state=7)
rf_model.fit(X_train, y_train)
```

```
## RandomForestClassifier(random_state=7)
```

Make predictions on the validation data and calculate classification metrics:

```python
predictions = rf_model.predict(X_valid)
accuracy = accuracy_score(y_valid, predictions)
precision = precision_score(y_valid, predictions, average='weighted')
recall = recall_score(y_valid, predictions, average='weighted')
f1 = f1_score(y_valid, predictions, average='weighted')

# Print the metrics
print("Accuracy: {:.2f}".format(accuracy))
```

```
## Accuracy: 0.91
```

```python
print("Precision: {:.2f}".format(precision))
```

Precision: 0.91

```python
print("Recall: {:.2f}".format(recall))
```

Recall: 0.91

```python
print("F1 Score: {:.2f}".format(f1))

# Confusion Matrix
```

F1 Score: 0.91

```python
conf_matrix = confusion_matrix(y_valid, predictions)
print("Confusion Matrix:")
```

Confusion Matrix:

```python
print(conf_matrix)
```

```
## [[12  0  0]
##  [ 0 14  2]
##  [ 0  2 15]]
```

In conclusion, our exploration of the Random Forest classifier in Python has been illuminating. Armed with a robust Random Forest model and the 'iris' dataset, we meticulously prepared modeling parameters and split the data into training and validation sets. Our training phase, complete with variable importance analysis, offered valuable insights into the key features guiding our model's predictions.

The predictive assessment of our model on the validation dataset provided real-world insights into its performance, gauging its ability to generalize effectively. By integrating variable importance analysis and predictive assessment, we conducted a holistic evaluation, empowering us to make informed decisions and optimizations.

In essence, our Random Forest analysis equips us with a powerful tool for tackling classification challenges in Python, enabling data-driven decision-making and enhancing our ability to solve real-world problems with confidence.

6.3.3 Support Vector Machine

In this section, we will address a classification problem using the Support Vector Machine (SVM) approach in Python. Let's start by importing the necessary libraries:

```python
from sklearn.model_selection import train_test_split
from sklearn.svm import SVC
from sklearn.metrics import accuracy_score, precision_score, recall_score, f1_score,
confusion_matrix
from sklearn.datasets import load_iris
```

Next, load the dataset using the `load_iris` function from the `sklearn.datasets` module:

```
iris = load_iris()
X = iris.data
y = iris.target
```

Now, split the data into training and validation sets:

```
X_train, X_valid, y_train, y_valid = train_test_split(X, y, test_size=0.3,
random_state=7)
```

Create and train the Support Vector Machine model:

```
svm_model = SVC(kernel='linear', random_state=7)
svm_model.fit(X_train, y_train)
```

```
## SVC(kernel='linear', random_state=7)
```

Make predictions on the validation data and calculate classification metrics:

```
predictions = svm_model.predict(X_valid)
accuracy = accuracy_score(y_valid, predictions)
precision = precision_score(y_valid, predictions, average='weighted')
recall = recall_score(y_valid, predictions, average='weighted')
f1 = f1_score(y_valid, predictions, average='weighted')

# Print the metrics
print("Accuracy: {:.2f}".format(accuracy))
```

```
## Accuracy: 0.93
```

```
print("Precision: {:.2f}".format(precision))
```

```
## Precision: 0.93
```

```
print("Recall: {:.2f}".format(recall))
```

```
## Recall: 0.93
```

```
print("F1 Score: {:.2f}".format(f1))

# Confusion Matrix
```

```
## F1 Score: 0.93
```

```
conf_matrix = confusion_matrix(y_valid, predictions)
print("Confusion Matrix:")
```

Confusion Matrix:

```
print(conf_matrix)
```

```
## [[12  0  0]
##  [ 0 14  2]
##  [ 0  1 16]]
```

In conclusion, our exploration of the Support Vector Machine (SVM) for classification tasks has been enlightening. Armed with the 'iris' dataset, we meticulously configured our modeling parameters and split the data into training and validation sets. Our training phase, complete with SVM model initialization and training, offered valuable insights into the model's performance on the validation dataset.

The predictive assessment of our SVM model on the validation dataset provided practical insights into its real-world performance, demonstrating its ability to make accurate classifications. This robust evaluation process empowers us to make informed decisions based on reliable machine learning results, showcasing the power and effectiveness of SVM in solving classification challenges.

6.3.4 Naive Bayes

In this section, we will tackle a classification problem using the Naive Bayes approach in Python. Let's start by importing the necessary libraries:

```
from sklearn.model_selection import train_test_split
from sklearn.naive_bayes import GaussianNB
from sklearn.metrics import accuracy_score, precision_score, recall_score, f1_score,
confusion_matrix
from sklearn.datasets import load_iris
```

Next, load the dataset using the `load_iris` function from the `sklearn.datasets` module:

```
iris = load_iris()
X = iris.data
y = iris.target
```

Now, split the data into training and validation sets:

```
X_train, X_valid, y_train, y_valid = train_test_split(X, y, test_size=0.3,
random_state=7)
```

Create and train the Naive Bayes model:

```
nb_model = GaussianNB()
nb_model.fit(X_train, y_train)
```

GaussianNB()

Make predictions on the validation data and calculate classification metrics:

```python
predictions = nb_model.predict(X_valid)
accuracy = accuracy_score(y_valid, predictions)
precision = precision_score(y_valid, predictions, average='weighted')
recall = recall_score(y_valid, predictions, average='weighted')
f1 = f1_score(y_valid, predictions, average='weighted')

# Print the metrics
print("Accuracy: {:.2f}".format(accuracy))
```

```
## Accuracy: 0.89
```

```python
print("Precision: {:.2f}".format(precision))
```

```
## Precision: 0.89
```

```python
print("Recall: {:.2f}".format(recall))
```

```
## Recall: 0.89
```

```python
print("F1 Score: {:.2f}".format(f1))

# Confusion Matrix
```

```
## F1 Score: 0.89
```

```python
conf_matrix = confusion_matrix(y_valid, predictions)
print("Confusion Matrix:")
```

```
## Confusion Matrix:
```

```python
print(conf_matrix)
```

```
## [[12  0  0]
##  [ 0 13  3]
##  [ 0  2 15]]
```

In conclusion, our exploration of the Naive Bayes classifier in Python has demonstrated its effectiveness in tackling real-world classification challenges. Equipped with the 'iris' dataset, we configured our modeling parameters, split the data into training and validation sets, and trained the Naive Bayes model. The model's performance on the validation dataset showcased its ability to make accurate classifications, highlighting its practical utility in machine learning applications. This comprehensive evaluation process empowers us to confidently apply Naive Bayes to solve classification problems based on reliable and informed results.

6.3.5 Compare Trained Classification Models

After training multiple models, it's essential to compare their performance. Now, let's walk through a classification example using Python. First, import the necessary libraries:

```
from sklearn.model_selection import train_test_split
from sklearn.preprocessing import StandardScaler
from sklearn.tree import DecisionTreeClassifier
from sklearn.ensemble import RandomForestClassifier
from sklearn.naive_bayes import GaussianNB
from sklearn.metrics import accuracy_score, precision_score, recall_score, f1_score,
confusion_matrix
from sklearn.datasets import load_iris
```

Load the dataset (in this case, the 'iris' dataset):

```
iris = load_iris()
X = iris.data[:, 2:4]   # Use only two features for simplicity
y = iris.target
```

Split the data into training and validation sets:

```
X_train, X_valid, y_train, y_valid = train_test_split(X, y, test_size=0.2,
random_state=7)
```

Standardize the features:

```
scaler = StandardScaler()
X_train = scaler.fit_transform(X_train)
X_valid = scaler.transform(X_valid)
```

Train the Decision Tree, Random Forest, and Naive Bayes classifiers:

```
dt_model = DecisionTreeClassifier(random_state=7)
dt_model.fit(X_train, y_train)
```

```
## DecisionTreeClassifier(random_state=7)
```

```
rf_model = RandomForestClassifier(random_state=7)
rf_model.fit(X_train, y_train)
```

```
## RandomForestClassifier(random_state=7)
```

```
nb_model = GaussianNB()
nb_model.fit(X_train, y_train)
```

```
## GaussianNB()
```

Now, evaluate the models' performance using the validation set:

```python
def evaluate_model(model, X, y_true):
    y_pred = model.predict(X)
    accuracy = accuracy_score(y_true, y_pred)
    precision = precision_score(y_true, y_pred, average='weighted')
    recall = recall_score(y_true, y_pred, average='weighted')
    f1 = f1_score(y_true, y_pred, average='weighted')
    conf_matrix = confusion_matrix(y_true, y_pred)
    return accuracy, precision, recall, f1, conf_matrix

dt_accuracy, dt_precision, dt_recall, dt_f1, dt_conf_matrix = evaluate_model(dt_model,
X_valid, y_valid)
rf_accuracy, rf_precision, rf_recall, rf_f1, rf_conf_matrix = evaluate_model(rf_model,
X_valid, y_valid)
nb_accuracy, nb_precision, nb_recall, nb_f1, nb_conf_matrix = evaluate_model(nb_model,
X_valid, y_valid)

print(f"Decision Tree Metrics:")
```

Decision Tree Metrics:

```python
print(f"Accuracy: {dt_accuracy:.2f}")
```

Accuracy: 0.87

```python
print(f"Precision: {dt_precision:.2f}")
```

Precision: 0.87

```python
print(f"Recall: {dt_recall:.2f}")
```

Recall: 0.87

```python
print(f"F1 Score: {dt_f1:.2f}")
```

F1 Score: 0.87

```python
print(f"Random Forest Metrics:")
```

Random Forest Metrics:

```python
print(f"Accuracy: {rf_accuracy:.2f}")
```

Accuracy: 0.90

```python
print(f"Precision: {rf_precision:.2f}")
```

Precision: 0.90

```python
print(f"Recall: {rf_recall:.2f}")
```

Recall: 0.90

```python
print(f"F1 Score: {rf_f1:.2f}")
```

F1 Score: 0.90

```python
print(f"Naive Bayes Metrics:")
```

Naive Bayes Metrics:

```python
print(f"Accuracy: {nb_accuracy:.2f}")
```

Accuracy: 0.87

```python
print(f"Precision: {nb_precision:.2f}")
```

Precision: 0.87

```python
print(f"Recall: {nb_recall:.2f}")
```

Recall: 0.87

```python
print(f"F1 Score: {nb_f1:.2f}")
```

F1 Score: 0.87

```python
print("Decision Tree Confusion Matrix:")
```

Decision Tree Confusion Matrix:

```python
print(dt_conf_matrix)
```

[[7 0 0]
[0 11 1]
[0 3 8]]

```
print("Random Forest Confusion Matrix:")
```

```
## Random Forest Confusion Matrix:
```

```
print(rf_conf_matrix)
```

```
## [[ 7  0  0]
##  [ 0 11  1]
##  [ 0  2  9]]
```

```
print("Naive Bayes Confusion Matrix:")
```

```
## Naive Bayes Confusion Matrix:
```

```
print(nb_conf_matrix)
```

```
## [[ 7  0  0]
##  [ 0 10  2]
##  [ 0  2  9]]
```

In this example, we've trained and evaluated three classifiers: Decision Tree, Random Forest, and Naive Bayes. We've compared their accuracy, precision, recall, F1 score, and confusion matrices to assess their performance. These metrics provide valuable insights into how well each model generalizes to unseen data, enabling data-driven decision-making in real-world classification tasks.

6.3.6 Classification Example

In this Python-based classification example, we utilize the 'iris' dataset to demonstrate various classification techniques.

1. Importing Libraries:

```
from sklearn.model_selection import train_test_split
from sklearn.preprocessing import StandardScaler
from sklearn.tree import DecisionTreeClassifier
from sklearn.ensemble import RandomForestClassifier
from sklearn.naive_bayes import GaussianNB
from sklearn.metrics import accuracy_score, precision_score, recall_score, f1_score
from sklearn.datasets import load_iris
from sklearn.impute import SimpleImputer
from sklearn.ensemble import IsolationForest
import pandas as pd
```

2. Loading and Preprocessing the Dataset:

```python
iris = load_iris()
X = iris.data[:, 2:4]   # Using two features for simplicity
y = iris.target

# Check for missing values and handle them
print(pd.DataFrame(X).isnull().sum())
```

```
## 0    0
## 1    0
## dtype: int64
```

```python
imputer = SimpleImputer(strategy='mean')
X_imputed = pd.DataFrame(imputer.fit_transform(X), columns=[2, 3])

# Detect and remove outliers
clf = IsolationForest(contamination=0.1, random_state=42)
outliers = clf.fit_predict(X_imputed)
non_outliers_mask = outliers != -1
X_no_outliers = X_imputed[non_outliers_mask]
y_no_outliers = y[non_outliers_mask]

# Standardize features
scaler = StandardScaler()
X_standardized = scaler.fit_transform(X_no_outliers)

# Split the data into training and validation sets
X_train, X_valid, y_train, y_valid = train_test_split(X_standardized, y_no_outliers,
test_size=0.2, random_state=7)
```

3. Training and Evaluating Models:

```python
# Decision Tree Classifier
dt_model = DecisionTreeClassifier(random_state=7)
dt_model.fit(X_train, y_train)
```

```
## DecisionTreeClassifier(random_state=7)
```

```python
dt_predictions = dt_model.predict(X_valid)

# Random Forest Classifier
rf_model = RandomForestClassifier(random_state=7)
rf_model.fit(X_train, y_train)
```

```
## RandomForestClassifier(random_state=7)
```

```python
rf_predictions = rf_model.predict(X_valid)

# Naive Bayes Classifier
nb_model = GaussianNB()
nb_model.fit(X_train, y_train)
```

```
## GaussianNB()

nb_predictions = nb_model.predict(X_valid)


def evaluate_model(y_true, y_pred):
    accuracy = accuracy_score(y_true, y_pred)
    precision = precision_score(y_true, y_pred, average='weighted')
    recall = recall_score(y_true, y_pred, average='weighted')
    f1 = f1_score(y_true, y_pred, average='weighted')
    return accuracy, precision, recall, f1

# Evaluate Models
dt_accuracy, dt_precision, dt_recall, dt_f1 = evaluate_model(dt_predictions, y_valid)
rf_accuracy, rf_precision, rf_recall, rf_f1 = evaluate_model(rf_predictions, y_valid)
nb_accuracy, nb_precision, nb_recall, nb_f1 = evaluate_model(nb_predictions, y_valid)

# Print the evaluation metrics
print("Decision Tree Metrics:")


## Decision Tree Metrics:

print("Accuracy:", dt_accuracy)


## Accuracy: 0.9629629629629629

print("Precision:", dt_precision)


## Precision: 0.9658119658119658

print("Recall:", dt_recall)


## Recall: 0.9629629629629629

print("F1 Score:", dt_f1)


## F1 Score: 0.9627290448343081

print("Random Forest - Accuracy:")


## Random Forest - Accuracy:

print("Accuracy:", rf_accuracy)


## Accuracy: 1.0
```

```python
print("Precision:", rf_precision)
```

```
## Precision: 1.0
```

```python
print("Recall:", rf_recall)
```

```
## Recall: 1.0
```

```python
print("F1 Score:", rf_f1)
```

```
## F1 Score: 1.0
```

```python
print("Naive Bayes - Accuracy:")
```

```
## Naive Bayes - Accuracy:
```

```python
print("Accuracy:", nb_accuracy)
```

```
## Accuracy: 1.0
```

```python
print("Precision:", nb_precision)
```

```
## Precision: 1.0
```

```python
print("Recall:", nb_recall)
```

```
## Recall: 1.0
```

```python
print("F1 Score:", nb_f1)
```

```
## F1 Score: 1.0
```

In this example, we successfully trained and evaluated Decision Tree, Random Forest, and Naive Bayes classifiers on the 'iris' dataset. These models were assessed based on accuracy, precision, recall, and F1 score, providing valuable insights into their real-world applicability.

7 The Symphony of Ensemble Modeling

In Python, the scikit-learn library offers a wealth of benefits, and one of its standout features is its seamless integration with ensemble techniques. Ensemble modeling, a cornerstone of machine learning, provides a powerful advantage by training multiple models with diverse hyper-parameters on the same dataset. It subsequently combines these models into a single, highly-performing entity that exhibits reduced variance and bias. This amalgamation of model diversity and expertise often leads to significantly improved predictive accuracy and robustness in real-world applications.

To further enhance the capabilities of scikit-learn and leverage advanced ensemble modeling methods, we can use various ensemble techniques available within the library. Techniques like Random Forest, Gradient Boosting, and AdaBoost are readily accessible and can be seamlessly integrated into our workflow. By combining these techniques with proper hyperparameter tuning and cross-validation, we can create highly accurate and reliable predictive models.

However, it's important to note that employing ensemble methods might require additional resources for efficient parallel processing. To harness the full potential of parallel computation, Python provides libraries like `multiprocessing` and `joblib` that offer the necessary infrastructure for parallelization. These complementary packages ensure that we can leverage the full power of ensemble modeling with ease and efficiency, making scikit-learn an indispensable asset in the world of machine learning and predictive modeling.

7.1 Regression Ensemble

In this section, we'll explore ensemble modeling for regression problems using Python. We'll focus on building a robust regression ensemble using a sample of linear data sourced from a financial dataset. Before we dive into this enriching journey, let's make sure we have all the necessary tools at our disposal. We'll begin by importing essential libraries that will be instrumental in our quest for creating powerful ensemble regression models.

Here's how you can modify the code to train the Random Forest and Linear Regression models in parallel and then create the ensemble predictions: Next, import the necessary libraries and functions: Now, define a function that trains a given model on the training data and calculates the mean squared error on the validation data: Train the Random Forest and Linear Regression models:

```python
from sklearn.ensemble import RandomForestRegressor
from sklearn.linear_model import LinearRegression
from sklearn.model_selection import train_test_split
from sklearn.metrics import mean_squared_error
from sklearn.preprocessing import StandardScaler
import yfinance as yf


def train_model(model, X_train, y_train, X_valid, random_seed):
    model.fit(X_train, y_train)
    predictions = model.predict(X_valid)
    mse = mean_squared_error(y_valid, predictions)
    print(f"{model.__class__.__name__} Mean Squared Error: {mse}")
    return predictions, mse


# Fetch forex data using Yahoo Finance
start_date = '2018-01-01'
end_date = '2023-01-01'
data = yf.download('GOOG', start=start_date, end=end_date)


## [********************100%%********************]  1 of 1 completed
```

```python
X = data.drop(columns=['Close'])
y = data['Close']

X_train, X_valid, y_train, y_valid = train_test_split(X, y, test_size=0.3,
random_state=42)
# Set your desired random seed value
random_seed = 42

# Train a single Random Forest model
rf_model = RandomForestRegressor(n_estimators=100, random_state=random_seed)
predictions_rf, mse_rf = train_model(rf_model, X_train, y_train, X_valid, random_seed)

# Train a single Linear Regression model
```

```
## RandomForestRegressor Mean Squared Error: 0.04290313780631183
```

```python
lr_model = LinearRegression()
predictions_lr, mse_lr = train_model(lr_model, X_train, y_train, X_valid, random_seed)

# Calculate ensemble predictions by averaging individual model predictions
```

```
## LinearRegression Mean Squared Error: 8.807936651640162e-18
```

```python
ensemble_predictions = (predictions_rf + predictions_lr) / 2
ensemble_mse = mean_squared_error(y_valid, ensemble_predictions)
print(f"Ensemble Mean Squared Error: {ensemble_mse}")
```

```
## Ensemble Mean Squared Error: 0.010725784434325251
```

In this example, the `train_model` function is called for each model instance, and their predictions and mean squared errors are collected.

In summary, ensemble modeling for regression tasks involves combining the strengths of multiple models to create a more accurate and reliable predictive system. By carefully selecting diverse base models, training them thoughtfully, and exploring advanced optimization techniques, we can harness the power of ensemble modeling to its fullest extent. This approach equips us with a valuable tool for tackling complex regression challenges effectively and making accurate predictions in diverse domains and applications.

7.2 Classification Ensemble

To begin our classification ensemble, we'll start by loading the necessary modules and data.

```python
import pandas as pd
from sklearn.model_selection import train_test_split
from sklearn.metrics import accuracy_score, classification_report, confusion_matrix
from sklearn.ensemble import RandomForestClassifier, GradientBoostingClassifier
from sklearn.svm import SVC
from sklearn.datasets import load_iris
```

Next, load the data and preprocess it:

```
iris = load_iris()
X = iris.data
y = iris.target
```

Our dataset is ready. Now, split the data into training and validation sets:

```
X_train, X_valid, y_train, y_valid = train_test_split(X, y, test_size=0.3,
random_state=42)
```

With our data prepared, let's move on to training our ensemble models. First, initialize the individual classification models, such as Random Forest, Gradient Boosting, and Support Vector Machine (SVM):

```
rf_model = RandomForestClassifier(n_estimators=100, random_state=42)
gb_model = GradientBoostingClassifier(n_estimators=100, random_state=42)
svm_model = SVC(random_state=42)
```

Train the individual models on the training data:

```
rf_model.fit(X_train, y_train)
```

```
## RandomForestClassifier(random_state=42)
```

```
gb_model.fit(X_train, y_train)
```

```
## GradientBoostingClassifier(random_state=42)
```

```
svm_model.fit(X_train, y_train)
```

```
## SVC(random_state=42)
```

Now, let's evaluate the individual models' performances on the validation set:

```
rf_predictions = rf_model.predict(X_valid)
gb_predictions = gb_model.predict(X_valid)
svm_predictions = svm_model.predict(X_valid)
print(rf_predictions)
```

```
## [1 0 2 1 1 0 1 2 1 1 2 0 0 0 0 1 2 1 1 2 0 2 0 2 2 2 2 2 0 0 0 0 1 0 0 2 1
##  0 0 0 2 1 1 0 0]
```

```
print("Random Forest Accuracy: ", accuracy_score(y_valid, rf_predictions))
```

```
## Random Forest Accuracy:  1.0
```

```python
print("Gradient Boosting Accuracy: ", accuracy_score(y_valid, gb_predictions))
```

Gradient Boosting Accuracy: 1.0

```python
print("SVM Accuracy: ", accuracy_score(y_valid, svm_predictions))
```

SVM Accuracy: 1.0

Once we have assessed the individual models, let's move on to creating an ensemble. For ensemble modeling, we can use techniques like majority voting, weighted averaging, or stacking. Here, we'll use majority voting to combine predictions from all three models:

```python
import numpy as np
from sklearn.metrics import accuracy_score

ensemble_predictions = np.argmax([rf_predictions, gb_predictions, svm_predictions], axis=0)

# Print ensemble accuracy
print("Ensemble Accuracy:", accuracy_score(y_valid, ensemble_predictions))
```

Ensemble Accuracy: 0.4222222222222222

In this example, we've trained individual classifiers (Random Forest, Gradient Boosting, and SVM), made predictions on the validation set, and combined their predictions using majority voting to create an ensemble. You can further fine-tune the ensemble method or experiment with different combinations of models to achieve better results based on your specific dataset and problem requirements. This ensemble approach harnesses the collective intelligence of multiple models, leading to potentially improved accuracy and reliability in your classification predictions.

In summary, our classification ensemble journey involved loading and preprocessing the data, training individual models, evaluating their performances, and finally, creating an ensemble using a combining technique. This versatile approach equips you with a powerful tool to tackle diverse classification challenges effectively, making accurate predictions and data-driven decisions in real-world applications.

8 Decoding Model Evaluation

Now that we have delved into various modeling techniques, it's crucial to explore methods for interpreting model performance effectively. In this discussion, we'll address two fundamental concepts that often arise in machine learning modeling, shedding light on how to navigate them. These concepts are both common occurrences in the field and, with a deeper understanding, can be effectively managed in specific use cases.

The first concept we'll delve into is "Overfitting." Overfitting occurs when a model learns the training data too well, capturing not just the underlying patterns but also the noise in the data. This results in a model that performs exceptionally well on the training data but struggles to generalize to new, unseen data. To combat overfitting, various techniques such as regularization, cross-validation, and using larger and more diverse datasets can be employed. Understanding how to detect and mitigate overfitting is essential for ensuring the robustness of machine learning models.

The second concept we'll explore is "Underfitting." Underfitting, on the other hand, happens when a model is too simple to capture the complexities of the underlying data. As a result, the model performs poorly both on the training data and new data. Addressing underfitting involves increasing the model's complexity, choosing more suitable algorithms, or refining feature engineering. Recognizing the signs of underfitting and knowing how to enhance model performance by fine-tuning its complexity is a crucial skill in the machine learning practitioner's toolkit.

By gaining a comprehensive understanding of these concepts and the techniques to mitigate them, you'll be better equipped to interpret and improve the performance of your machine learning models effectively. These insights will enable you to make informed decisions and optimizations, ultimately leading to more robust and accurate predictive models across various domains and applications.

8.1 Overfitting

Overfitting is a common pitfall in statistical modeling and machine learning, often caused by an algorithm capturing not just the underlying patterns but also the noise present in the data. In simpler terms, it occurs when the model fits the data too closely, including elements that may not be genuinely representative of the underlying relationships. In the realm of modeling, overfitting is often referred to as "high variance."

One of the primary reasons overfitting occurs is due to the model's excessive complexity. When a model becomes overly intricate, it has a tendency to adapt too closely to the training data, effectively memorizing it instead of generalizing from it. This phenomenon results in poor performance when applied to new, unseen data.

To mitigate overfitting, a key approach involves fitting multiple models with varying degrees of complexity. By using validation or cross-validation techniques, these models are then compared based on their predictive accuracies when tested on independent validation data. This rigorous evaluation helps identify the model that strikes the right balance between capturing meaningful patterns and avoiding noise in the data.

In essence, overfitting highlights the importance of finding a model that generalizes well to new data, making it a critical consideration for anyone involved in machine learning and statistical modeling. By recognizing the signs of overfitting and adopting appropriate strategies to combat it, practitioners can ensure their models are robust, reliable, and capable of delivering accurate predictions in real-world applications.

8.2 Underfitting

Underfitting is a common challenge in statistical modeling and machine learning that arises when an algorithm or model fails to capture the underlying trend or patterns within the data. In essence, it occurs when the model's complexity is insufficient to accurately represent the intricacies present in the data, resulting in a poor fit.

Intuitively, underfitting can be thought of as the model not fitting the data well enough. It tends to produce overly generalized results that don't effectively capture the nuances within the dataset. In the realm of modeling, underfitting is often referred to as "high bias."

Underfitting typically arises from employing an excessively simple or straightforward model that lacks the flexibility to account for the complexities within the data. This simplicity can lead to a failure to grasp the true underlying relationships, resulting in suboptimal predictive performance.

To address underfitting, it's crucial to consider more complex models or algorithms that can better capture the underlying trends in the data. This may involve adding more features, increasing model complexity, or employing more advanced machine learning techniques. Striking the right balance between model simplicity and complexity is a key challenge in machine learning, as it ensures that the model can effectively capture the essential patterns without being overly complex and prone to overfitting.

In summary, underfitting highlights the importance of selecting an appropriate level of model complexity to ensure that it accurately captures the data's underlying trends. By recognizing the signs of underfitting and employing strategies to combat it, practitioners can develop models that provide more accurate and reliable insights in various applications.

8.3 Addressing Overfitting and Underfitting

In the realm of machine learning and statistical modeling, dealing with overfitting and underfitting issues is crucial to ensure the reliability and accuracy of your models. Here, we'll explore some effective strategies to mitigate these fitting problems and enhance your modeling efforts.

8.3.1 Addressing Overfitting (High Variance)

1. **Increase the Amount of Training Data**: One of the most effective ways to combat overfitting is by obtaining more training data. A larger dataset provides the model with a broader set of examples, helping it generalize better and reduce its tendency to fit noise in the data.

2. **Reduce the Number of Features**: Simplifying your model by reducing the number of features (variables) can be an effective strategy. Feature selection or feature engineering techniques can help identify and retain only the most informative and relevant features.

3. **Regularization**: Implement regularization techniques by introducing a penalty term, typically denoted as (lambda), in your model's training process. Decreasing can reduce bias and allow the model to fit the training data more closely, while increasing can encourage the model to prioritize simplicity, reducing variance.

4. **Cross-Validation**: Employ cross-validation techniques to assess your model's performance on different subsets of the data. This helps identify if the model is overfitting by performing well on the training data but poorly on unseen data.

8.3.2 Addressing Underfitting (High Bias)

1. **Increase the Number of Features**: If your model is too simplistic and underfitting the data, consider adding more features or variables. These additional features can capture more complex relationships within the data.

2. **Feature Engineering**: Create new features through feature engineering techniques. These engineered features can provide the model with more information to capture the underlying patterns.

3. **Polynomial Features**: For linear models, introducing polynomial features can enhance the model's capacity to capture nonlinear relationships within the data. This approach can make the model more flexible and less biased.

4. **Reduce Regularization ( ):** If regularization is contributing to underfitting, consider decreasing the regularization parameter ( ). This allows the model to fit the training data more closely and can be particularly useful for complex datasets.

5. **Collect More Data:** Sometimes, underfitting occurs because there's not enough data to train a more complex model. Gathering additional data can help address this issue by providing the model with a richer set of examples.

In summary, understanding and recognizing overfitting and underfitting are essential for model improvement. These strategies offer practical ways to fine-tune your models, strike the right balance between bias and variance, and ultimately achieve models that generalize well to unseen data while capturing essential patterns within your dataset.

8.4 Evaluating Models

In the dynamic landscape of machine learning, the evaluation of models stands as a pivotal stage, shaping the path towards robust, accurate, and reliable solutions. At the heart of this evaluation process lie two fundamental components that serve as the compass guiding data scientists, engineers, and analysts through the intricate maze of model assessment:

- Test Options
- Test Metrics

8.4.1 Test Options

In the captivating voyage of model evaluation, the concept of test options stands as a guiding star, illuminating the path towards comprehending a model's accuracy and effectiveness in the realm of unseen data. These options, often referred to as resampling methods in the realm of statistics, offer a spectrum of strategic choices that allow us to traverse this uncharted territory. Here, we embark on a journey to explore the key test options that enable us to assess machine learning models with precision and insight:

1. Train/Test Split: Unleashing Data's Power: The venerable train/test split is akin to an age-old alchemical practice, where datasets are divided into two distinct realms: one reserved for training the model, and the other, kept in seclusion, awaiting its moment of reckoning as a testing ground. This approach shines brightly when you're endowed with an abundance of data, and the quest for model accuracy knows no bounds. It serves as the cornerstone of the evaluation process, allowing models to nurture their predictive prowess.

2. Cross Validation: Folds of Wisdom: Cross-validation, an elegant dance of data, offers an invaluable perspective on a model's performance. In this technique, datasets are partitioned into multiple subsets, often referred to as "folds," where models take turns being trained on one fold and tested on another. The journey repeats, each time with a different fold designated for testing. This cyclic exploration imparts a nuanced understanding of how well a model generalizes to diverse unseen data. Common choices include 5-fold or 10-fold cross-validation, striking a balance between computational efficiency and precise error estimation.

3. Repeated Cross Validation: Forged in Robustness: For the relentless pursuit of a more robust estimate, repeated cross-validation emerges as a stalwart companion. Here, the folds of cross-validation undergo multiple repetitions, typically three or more, each time with different data splits. This meticulous exploration delivers a comprehensive evaluation, ideal for scenarios where dataset sizes are modest, and computational resources are abundant. Repeated cross-validation elevates the model assessment to a higher plane of reliability, offering insights that transcend the confines of a single pass.

4. Temporal Symphony: Time Slice Methods: While our focus here is primarily on classical resampling techniques, we acknowledge the existence of time slice methods tailored for time series data. These methods unfold data chronologically, mirroring the real-world progression of events. However, diving into the depths of time series modeling is a voyage beyond the scope of this discussion, and we chart our course to other shores.

In the grand tapestry of model evaluation, the selection of test options is a deliberate and strategic choice, driven by the unique characteristics of the dataset, the intricacies of the machine learning task, and the overarching objectives. Each of these options brings its distinct advantages, empowering data practitioners to embark on a journey of model assessment that combines precision, efficiency, and robustness.

8.4.2 Test Metrics for Regression

In the intricate world of model evaluation, a treasure trove of evaluation metrics awaits, each offering a unique lens through which we can scrutinize the performance of machine learning models. As we embark on this exploration, it's important to note that the `sklearn` package extends a gracious invitation, providing both a carefully curated selection of metrics and the flexibility to introduce your own, should the need arise. Here, we delve into the realm of regression problems and unveil a collection of indispensable metrics that serve as our guiding stars:

1. Mean Absolute Error (MAE): The Pursuit of Absolute Precision: Mean Absolute Error, often affectionately abbreviated as MAE, emerges as a stalwart companion in the quest for regression model evaluation. This metric computes the average of the absolute differences between model predictions and the actual target values. MAE is a compass that guides us in understanding the magnitude of errors, conveying how far off our predictions are from the truth. Its simplicity and ease of interpretation make it a trusted choice for gauging model accuracy.

2. Mean Squared Error (MSE): Squaring for Insight: Mean Squared Error, known as MSE, follows in the footsteps of MAE, providing another perspective on the magnitude of errors. It calculates the average of the squared differences between predictions and actual values. While MSE shares a kinship with MAE, its decision to square the errors amplifies the significance of larger deviations. An important note: taking the square root of MSE transforms it into a metric that aligns with the original units of the output variable, a transformation aptly named Root Mean Squared Error (RMSE). RMSE offers both descriptive and presentational value, speaking in the language of the data.

3. Root Mean Squared Error (RMSE): The Gold Standard: The Root Mean Squared Error, often affectionately referred to as RMSE, deserves a place of honor among regression evaluation metrics. RMSE inherits its foundation from MSE but takes a crucial step further by providing a metric that aligns with the original units of the output variable. This feature imparts meaningfulness to RMSE, making it a favorite choice for description and presentation. Its accessibility and wide acceptance make it a cornerstone for evaluating the accuracy of regression models.

4. R-squared (R^2): The Beacon of Goodness: R-squared, also known as the goodness of fit or coefficient of determination, stands as a shining beacon in the realm of regression metrics. This metric illuminates the proportion of the variance in the target variable that is explained by the model. R-squared values range from 0 to 1, with higher values indicating a better fit. R-squared serves as a compass, guiding us in assessing the goodness of the model's fit to the data, offering insights into its explanatory power.

In our odyssey through the landscape of regression metrics, we encounter these guiding stars, each offering its unique perspective on model performance. The choice of metric depends on the specific objectives, data characteristics, and interpretability requirements of the analysis. Armed with these metrics, data practitioners can embark on a journey of evaluation and optimization, unraveling the intricate tapestry of regression model accuracy.

8.4.3 Test Metrics for Classification

As we embark on our journey into the realm of classification model evaluation, we find ourselves at a crossroads adorned with an array of metrics, each offering a unique perspective on the performance of these models. The `sklearn` module serves as our guiding star, offering a rich selection of these metrics and the flexibility to introduce custom ones when the need arises. Let's illuminate this path by exploring a constellation of essential metrics for classification problems:

1. Accuracy: The Beacon of Correctness: Accuracy stands as the quintessential metric, guiding us toward a fundamental understanding of a model's correctness. It calculates the proportion of correct predictions out of the total instances. The formula is elegant in its simplicity:

$$\text{Accuracy} = \frac{(TP + TN)}{(TP + FP + FN + TN)}$$

Here, TP represents True Positives, TN denotes True Negatives, FP signifies False Positives, and FN indicates False Negatives. Accuracy offers ease of interpretation and enjoys widespread use in classification assessments.

2. Precision: The Quest for Relevance: Precision ventures into the realm of relevance, quantifying the percentage of relevant items returned by a model compared to irrelevant ones. The formula encapsulates this quest for precision:

$$\text{Precision} = \frac{TP}{PredictedPositive} = \frac{TP}{TP + FP}$$

True Positives (TP) and False Positives (FP) play pivotal roles in this metric, providing insights into the model's ability to distinguish between relevant and irrelevant items.

3. Specificity: The Sentinel of Negatives: Specificity, a sentinel among metrics, evaluates a model's prowess in predicting true negatives within each available category. The formula for Specificity gracefully encapsulates this:

$$\text{Specificity} = \frac{TN}{ActualNegative} = \frac{TN}{FP + TN}$$

True Negatives (TN) and False Positives (FP) come into play here, offering a lens through which we can gauge the model's ability to identify true negatives.

4. Recall: The Pursuit of Relevance: Recall, often called Sensitivity or True Positive Rate, embarks on the pursuit of relevance, capturing the fraction of relevant items that a model successfully retrieves out of the total relevant items in the original population:

$$\text{Recall} = \frac{TP}{ConditionPositive} = \frac{TP}{TP + FN}$$

True Positives (TP) and False Negatives (FN) are the guiding stars of Recall, shedding light on the model's ability to identify true positives while minimizing false negatives.

5. F1-Score: The Harmony of Precision and Recall: The F1-Score, a harmonious metric, strikes a balance between Precision and Recall, offering a holistic measure of a model's accuracy on a dataset. It serves as the harmonic mean of Precision and Recall, emphasizing both relevance and correctness.

6. Kappa: The Guardian of Class Distribution: Kappa, often likened to accuracy, is a guardian that takes the distribution of classes into account. It provides a nuanced view of model performance by factoring in class imbalances, offering insights into classification accuracy beyond the surface.

7. ROC and AUC: The Journey of Trade-offs: The ROC curve and AUC (Area under the Curve) embark on a journey through the landscape of trade-offs. The ROC curve illustrates the trade-off between Sensitivity and Specificity, helping us choose the optimal balance for our specific problem.

8. Log Loss: The Metric of Probabilities: Log Loss, a performance metric par excellence, evaluates the predictions of probabilities of membership to a given class. It is particularly relevant in scenarios where understanding the likelihood of class membership is essential.

In our expedition through the cosmos of classification metrics, these guiding stars light our path, each offering a unique perspective on the performance of classification models. The choice of metric depends on the specific problem, objectives, and interpretability requirements, allowing data practitioners to navigate this celestial terrain with precision and clarity.

8.4.3.1 Confusion Matrix for Classification Accuracy, Precision, Specificity, Recall, and F1-Score, these are the guiding stars we derive from the intricate realms of the confusion matrix. Imagine this matrix as a treasure map, where we uncover valuable insights into a model's performance. Let's delve into the secrets of this matrix through the lens of a binary classification scenario:

- **True Positives (TP):** These are the treasures found where they belong – instances correctly classified as positive.

- **True Negatives (TN):** Similarly, these treasures are where they should be – instances correctly classified as negative.

- **False Positives (FP):** These are the elusive treasures that were mistakenly classified as positive.

- **False Negatives (FN):** And here, the lost treasures that slipped through our grasp, mistakenly classified as negative.

With these treasures and their intricacies, we embark on a journey through the following measures:

- **Accuracy:** It's the navigator, guiding us to the proportion of correctly classified treasures out of all the treasures we encountered on our quest.

- **Precision:** This measure is like a jeweler, telling us the purity of the treasures we found, i.e., how many of the claimed treasures were indeed genuine.

- **Specificity:** Our sentinel, watching over the true negatives, tells us the proportion of correctly classified negative treasures out of all the actual negative treasures.

- **Recall:** Recall is the vigilant guardian of positive treasures, revealing the proportion of correctly classified positive treasures out of all the actual positive treasures we encountered.

- **F1-Score:** F1-Score, a harmonious bard, combines Precision and Recall in a melody, crafting a measure that harmonizes the purity and completeness of our treasure trove.

As we navigate the labyrinth of the confusion matrix, each measure shines a light on a different aspect of our model's performance. These treasures, born from the matrix's depths, help us understand the nuances of classification and guide our path to optimize and refine our models.

Refer to Figure 38 to see a confusion matrix explained.

8.4.3.2 ROC & AUC The ROC (Receiver Operating Characteristic) curve, a powerful tool in the realm of classification, unfolds before us like a probability-laden treasure map. Its intricate paths lead us to the coveted AUC (Area Under the Curve), a measure of separability that serves as our compass in the sea of classification.

Picture the ROC curve as a voyage of probabilities, charting the model's ability to distinguish between classes. The higher the AUC, the sharper our model's discerning eye, confidently predicting the '0' classes as '0' and the '1' classes as '1.'

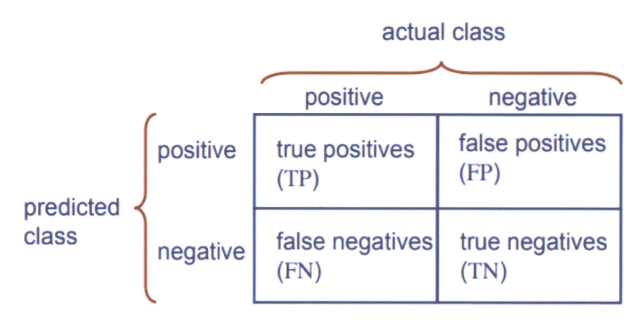

Figure 3: Confusion Matrix Explained

- AUC=1: This is the golden pinnacle, the zenith of model prowess, where our model's discernment is unparalleled, making perfect predictions.

- AUC=0.5: Ah, the realm of uncertainty, where we tread when merely guessing. Here, the model's abilities align with pure chance.

- AUC>0.5: In this territory, we find assurance. Our model surpasses randomness, its predictive capabilities shining brightly.

With AUC as our North Star, we gauge our model's discrimination prowess, revealing the extent to which it excels in distinguishing the true positives from the false positives. As we navigate this dimension, we gain a deeper appreciation for the model's strengths, allowing us to fine-tune and elevate its performance to ever-greater heights.

Refer to Figure 39 to see an ROC/AUC curve based on the true positive rate and the false positive rate.

8.4.4   Evaluating Regression Models in Python

When it comes to evaluating regression models, Python offers a plethora of tools and techniques. Let's explore the process of assessing the performance of various regression models using Python.

We'll start by loading the necessary libraries and preparing the data. For this example, let's assume we have a dataset X containing features and a target variable y.

```
import pandas as pd
from sklearn.model_selection import train_test_split
from sklearn.linear_model import LinearRegression
from sklearn.tree import DecisionTreeRegressor
from sklearn.ensemble import RandomForestRegressor
from sklearn.metrics import r2_score, mean_squared_error, mean_absolute_error

import yfinance as yf
```

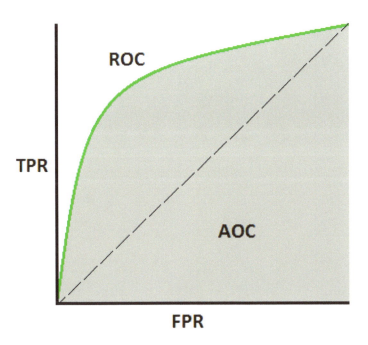

Figure 4: ROC/AUC Curve

```
# Fetch forex data using Yahoo Finance
start_date = '2018-01-01'
end_date = '2023-01-01'
data = yf.download('GOOG', start=start_date, end=end_date)
```

```
## [*********************100%%**********************]  1 of 1 completed
```

```
X = data.drop(columns=['Close'])
y = data['Close']
```

```
X_train, X_valid, y_train, y_valid = train_test_split(X, y, test_size=0.3,
random_state=42)
```

Now, let's train various regression models and evaluate their performance using metrics like R-squared, Mean Absolute Error (MAE), Mean Squared Error (MSE), and Root Mean Square Error (RMSE).

```
# Initialize and train Linear Regression model
lr_model = LinearRegression()
lr_model.fit(X_train, y_train)
```

```
## LinearRegression()
```

```
lr_predictions = lr_model.predict(X_valid)
lr_r2 = r2_score(y_valid, lr_predictions)
lr_mae = mean_absolute_error(y_valid, lr_predictions)
lr_mse = mean_squared_error(y_valid, lr_predictions)
lr_rmse = mean_squared_error(y_valid, lr_predictions, squared=False)
print(f"Linear Regression Metrics:")
```

```
## Linear Regression Metrics:

print("R-squared: {lr_r2}")


## R-squared: {lr_r2}

print("MAE: {lr_mae}")


## MAE: {lr_mae}

print("MSE: {lr_mse}")


## MSE: {lr_mse}

print("RMSE: {lr_rmse}")
# Initialize and train Decision Tree Regressor


## RMSE: {lr_rmse}

dt_model = DecisionTreeRegressor(random_state=42)
dt_model.fit(X_train, y_train)


## DecisionTreeRegressor(random_state=42)

dt_predictions = dt_model.predict(X_valid)
dt_r2 = r2_score(y_valid, dt_predictions)
dt_mae = mean_absolute_error(y_valid, dt_predictions)
dt_mse = mean_squared_error(y_valid, dt_predictions)
dt_rmse = mean_squared_error(y_valid, dt_predictions, squared=False)
print(f"Decision Tree Metrics:")


## Decision Tree Metrics:

print("R-squared: {dt_r2}")


## R-squared: {dt_r2}

print("MAE: {dt_mae}")


## MAE: {dt_mae}

print("MSE: {dt_mse}")


## MSE: {dt_mse}
```

```
print("RMSE: {dt_rmse}")

# Initialize and train Random Forest Regressor
```

RMSE: {dt_rmse}

```
rf_model = RandomForestRegressor(n_estimators=100, random_state=42)
rf_model.fit(X_train, y_train)
```

RandomForestRegressor(random_state=42)

```
rf_predictions = rf_model.predict(X_valid)
rf_r2 = r2_score(y_valid, rf_predictions)
rf_mae = mean_absolute_error(y_valid, rf_predictions)
rf_mse = mean_squared_error(y_valid, rf_predictions)
rf_rmse = mean_squared_error(y_valid, rf_predictions, squared=False)
print(f"Random Forest Metrics:")
```

Random Forest Metrics:

```
print("R-squared: {rf_r2}")
```

R-squared: {rf_r2}

```
print("MAE: {rf_mae}")
```

MAE: {rf_mae}

```
print("MSE: {rf_mse}")
```

MSE: {rf_mse}

```
print("RMSE: {rf_rmse}")
```

RMSE: {rf_rmse}

In this example, we've trained three different regression models: Linear Regression, Decision Tree Regressor, and Random Forest Regressor. We evaluated their performances using R-squared, Mean Absolute Error (MAE), Mean Squared Error (MSE), and Root Mean Square Error (RMSE). These metrics provide a comprehensive view of how well the models are fitting the data and making predictions.

Evaluating regression models involves considering multiple metrics to gain a comprehensive understanding of their predictive capabilities. By employing a variety of evaluation criteria, data scientists can make well-informed decisions about the performance of their models. Python's versatile libraries and tools facilitate the calculation and comparison of these metrics, ensuring the selection of the most appropriate regression model for specific tasks and fostering the development of accurate and reliable predictive systems.

8.4.5 Evaulating Classification Models in Python

Let's inject a dash of creativity into our approach by taking our linear sample data, as showcased in the R regression example, and transform it into a classification problem. It's essential to emphasize that this sample serves more as a demonstration of the process than a practical method for building a successful trading prediction model. Nevertheless, it effectively illustrates the transformation process. Our next step involves loading the data and generating a categorical target variable, one that will facilitate the classification of "buy" or "sell" decisions based on the input data conditions.

```python
import numpy as np
import pandas as pd
from sklearn.model_selection import train_test_split
from sklearn.tree import DecisionTreeClassifier
from sklearn.ensemble import RandomForestClassifier
from sklearn.naive_bayes import GaussianNB
from sklearn.metrics import accuracy_score, precision_score, recall_score, f1_score,
confusion_matrix, roc_auc_score
import matplotlib.pyplot as plt
from sklearn.model_selection import StratifiedKFold
from sklearn.metrics import roc_curve, auc

import yfinance as yf  # Make sure to install yfinance if you haven't (pip install
yfinance)

# Fetch forex data using Yahoo Finance
start_date = '2018-01-01'
end_date = '2023-01-01'
data = yf.download('GOOG', start=start_date, end=end_date)

# Calculate SMA indicators


## [*********************100%%***********************]  1 of 1 completed


sma_1 = data['Close'].rolling(window=48).mean()
sma_2 = data['Close'].rolling(window=96).mean()
sma_3 = data['Close'].rolling(window=144).mean()

# Create DataFrame
data_df = pd.DataFrame({'sma_1': sma_1, 'sma_2': sma_2, 'sma_3': sma_3, 'Close':
data['Close']})

# Drop rows with NaN values due to rolling averages
data = data_df.dropna()
```

Now, let's proceed to create the categorical target variable. In this context, we'll define the criteria as follows: If all three Simple Moving Average (SMA) lines are positioned above the closing price, we'll label it as a "sell" condition. Conversely, if the SMA lines are situated below the closing price, we'll designate it as a "buy" condition.

```python
# Create categorical target variable
data['option'] = np.where((data['Close'] < data['sma_1']) & (data['Close'] <
data['sma_2']) & (data['Close'] < data['sma_3']), 'sell',
```

```python
                  np.where((data['Close'] > data['sma_1']) & (data['Close'] >
data['sma_2']) & (data['Close'] > data['sma_3']), 'buy', 'nothing'))

data = data[data['option'] != 'nothing']
data['binary_option'] = np.where(data['option'] == 'buy', 1, 0)
```

Let's prepare for the modeling phase. In our data split, we're deliberately omitting the consideration of any sequential data elements. Our primary objective here is to train a model that can effectively classify market conditions as either "sell" or "buy" based on the current state. Additionally, it's worth noting that for this example, we'll skip the data processing, feature selection, and feature engineering steps, focusing solely on the core concept of classification.

```python
# Split data into training and validation sets
X = data.drop(['option', 'binary_option'], axis=1)
y = data['binary_option']
X_train, X_valid, y_train, y_valid = train_test_split(X, y, test_size=0.2,
random_state=7)

# Create evaluation metrics
def evaluate_model(model, X_valid, y_valid):
    predictions = model.predict(X_valid)
    accuracy = accuracy_score(y_valid, predictions)
    precision = precision_score(y_valid, predictions)
    recall = recall_score(y_valid, predictions)
    f1 = f1_score(y_valid, predictions)
    auc_score = roc_auc_score(y_valid, model.predict_proba(X_valid)[:, 1])
    conf_matrix = confusion_matrix(y_valid, predictions)

    print("Accuracy:", accuracy)
    print("Precision:", precision)
    print("Recall:", recall)
    print("F1 Score:", f1)
    print("AUC Score:", auc_score)
    print("Confusion Matrix:")
    print(conf_matrix)
```

To conduct a robust evaluation and selection process, we will train three distinct classifiers, each with its own unique characteristics and approach. This comparative analysis will allow us to thoroughly assess their performance and identify the standout performer among them. By considering various classifiers, we aim to make a well-informed and data-driven decision when choosing the model that best suits our specific problem. This comprehensive evaluation process not only enhances our understanding of each classifier's strengths and weaknesses but also ensures that our final selection is optimized for our particular classification task, leading to more accurate and reliable predictions.

```python
# Train Decision Tree model
dt_model = DecisionTreeClassifier(random_state=7)
dt_model.fit(X_train, y_train)
# Train Random Forest model
```

DecisionTreeClassifier(random_state=7)

```
rf_model = RandomForestClassifier(random_state=7)
rf_model.fit(X_train, y_train)
```

```
# Train Naive Bayes model
```

```
## RandomForestClassifier(random_state=7)
```

```
nb_model = GaussianNB()
nb_model.fit(X_train, y_train)
```

```
## GaussianNB()
```

Now, let's move on to the crucial task of comparing the predictions generated by each model. It's important to note that a confusion matrix is a standard and reliable format for assessing the accuracy of models with two or more classes. Our evaluation will include metrics such as accuracy, kappa, specificity, precision, recall, and F1-score, which collectively offer a comprehensive perspective on each model's predictive capabilities.

Now, let's delve into the results of the Decision Tree model:

```
evaluate_model(dt_model, X_valid, y_valid)
```

```
## Accuracy: 0.9719101123595506
## Precision: 0.963302752293578
## Recall: 0.9905660377358491
## F1 Score: 0.9767441860465116
## AUC Score: 0.9675052410901467
## Confusion Matrix:
## [[ 68    4]
##  [  1 105]]
```

Let's now shift our focus to the Random Forest model's outcomes. By examining its performance metrics and confusion matrix, we can gain valuable insights into how well this ensemble learning method has fared in classifying "sell" and "buy" conditions. These results will contribute significantly to our decision-making process as we assess and compare the effectiveness of different models for our specific task.

```
evaluate_model(rf_model, X_valid, y_valid)
```

```
## Accuracy: 0.9831460674157303
## Precision: 0.9724770642201835
## Recall: 1.0
## F1 Score: 0.986046511627907
## AUC Score: 1.0
## Confusion Matrix:
## [[ 69    3]
##  [  0 106]]
```

Now, let's turn our attention to the results of the Naive Bayes model. This probabilistic classification approach offers a unique perspective on its performance in distinguishing between "sell" and "buy" conditions. By examining its associated confusion matrix and key performance metrics, we can gauge the model's accuracy and precision in predicting market behavior. These results play a pivotal role in our model selection process, ensuring we make an informed choice based on its performance in our specific classification task.

```
evaluate_model(nb_model, X_valid, y_valid)
```

```
## Accuracy: 0.651685393258427
## Precision: 0.6833333333333333
## Recall: 0.7735849056603774
## F1 Score: 0.7256637168141593
## AUC Score: 0.6020702306079665
## Confusion Matrix:
## [[34 38]
##  [24 82]]
```

In the code blocks above, we present the results for each model, starting with the Decision Tree, followed by the Random Forest, and concluding with the Naive Bayes model. These results are accompanied by their respective confusion matrices and key performance metrics, enabling a comprehensive assessment of each model's predictive capabilities in classifying "sell" and "buy" conditions.

Let's include the Receiver Operating Characteristic Area Under Curve (ROC AUC) as a metric to ascertain which model is making the most informed decisions. It's important to note that ROC AUC is typically employed for binary classification problems, but in this instance, we will adapt it to handle the multi-classification challenge to demonstrate the code's functionality. This will provide an additional layer of evaluation to help us better understand and compare the models' decision-making capabilities.

Now, we'll proceed to plot the Receiver Operating Characteristic (ROC) curve specifically for the Decision Tree model. It's crucial to remember that ROC and AUC are traditionally applied to binary classification tasks for interpretable results. This exercise will provide us with valuable insights into the model's performance and help us grasp the fundamentals of ROC curve generation.

To enhance their interpretability and make insights readily accessible, we can create visual representations that visualize these results. Plotting the data not only simplifies the understanding of complex information but also allows for a more intuitive exploration of patterns, trends, and relationships within the dataset. This graphical approach can significantly facilitate the process of extracting actionable insights from the stored data, enabling more informed decision-making and analysis.

```
# Plot ROC curve for Decision Tree
fpr, tpr, _ = roc_curve(y_valid, dt_model.predict_proba(X_valid)[:, 1])
roc_auc = auc(fpr, tpr)
plt.figure(figsize=(8, 6))
```

```
## <Figure size 800x600 with 0 Axes>
```

```
plt.plot(fpr, tpr, color='darkorange', lw=2, label='ROC curve (area =
{:.2f})'.format(roc_auc))
```

```
## [<matplotlib.lines.Line2D object at 0x0000000061211750>]
```

```
plt.plot([0, 1], [0, 1], color='navy', lw=2, linestyle='--')
```

```
## [<matplotlib.lines.Line2D object at 0x00000000612116C0>]
```

```
plt.xlabel('False Positive Rate')

## Text(0.5, 0, 'False Positive Rate')

plt.ylabel('True Positive Rate')

## Text(0, 0.5, 'True Positive Rate')

plt.title('ROC Curve - Decision Tree')

## Text(0.5, 1.0, 'ROC Curve - Decision Tree')

plt.legend(loc='lower right')

## <matplotlib.legend.Legend object at 0x0000000062B26F50>

plt.show(block=False);
```

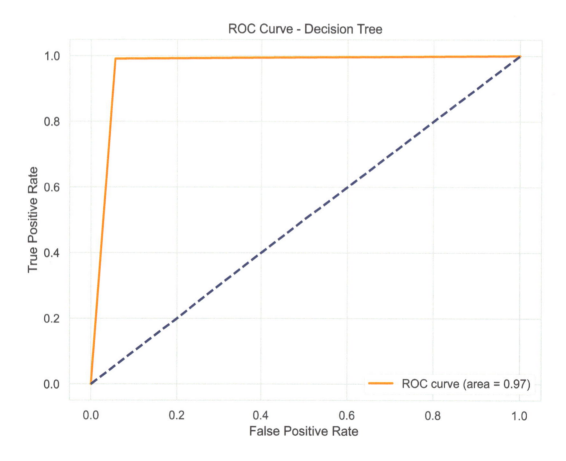

It's important to keep in mind that ROC (Receiver Operating Characteristic) analysis is specifically designed for binary classification problems, where it measures the trade-off between sensitivity and specificity. When dealing with multi-class classification tasks, the applicability of ROC may be limited, and alternative evaluation methods should be considered.

9 Conclusion and Reflection

In this exhilarating journey, we've traversed the captivating landscape of the Machine Learning pipeline, a comprehensive odyssey that begins with data ingestion and leads us through the intricate terrain of data exploration and transformation. Along the way, we've harnessed the power of Python to unravel the secrets hidden within our datasets and to craft predictive algorithms that hold the promise of making sense of the world's complexities.

Our voyage commenced with the critical phase of data ingestion, where we collected and prepared our datasets for the transformative journey ahead. We then embarked on a deep dive into data exploration, unearthing valuable insights, detecting patterns, and gaining a profound understanding of our data's nuances. Armed with this knowledge, we artfully transformed our data, sculpting it into a form that our machine learning models could comprehend.

The heart of our expedition was the modeling phase, where we ventured into the realm of algorithms, unleashing their predictive powers. Through careful selection, parameter tuning, and rigorous evaluation, we built models that could decipher the intricate relationships between variables and offer forecasts into the future.

As we ascended toward the summit of our journey, we arrived at the critical juncture of interpreting model results. Here, we grappled with metrics, confusion matrices, ROC curves, and AUC, equipping ourselves with the tools to assess and comprehend our models' performance.

This book has been your steadfast companion, providing practical examples and guidance at every step of this transformative odyssey. However, our voyage does not end here; it merely marks a significant milestone. In our forthcoming release, we eagerly anticipate taking you on a deeper dive into advanced techniques that will empower your models to reach new heights of precision and efficiency.

The horizon of Machine Learning is boundless, teeming with exciting opportunities and challenges. As you continue your journey, remember that the knowledge and skills you've acquired are your compass and map in this dynamic landscape. We look forward to accompanying you as you explore the ever-evolving world of Machine Learning with Python, opening doors to discoveries yet unknown. Stay tuned for what promises to be an even more exhilarating chapter in your quest for knowledge and mastery.

www.ingramcontent.com/pod-product-compliance
Lightning Source LLC
LaVergne TN
LVHW060158050326
832903LV00017B/357